Mo

The Allure of Mo...

By Jon Miller

This book is adapted from, inspired by and contains verbatim selections from *The Mountain* by Jules Michelet; *Ascent to the summit of Mont Blanc 1834* By Martin Barry; *Narrative of an ascent to the summit of Mont Blanc* By John Auldjo; *Chamonix and the range of Mont Blanc: a guide* By Edward Whymper; and *the 40th Ascent to Mont Blanc* by Paul Verne, *As a man Thinketh* by James Allen and *Nature or The Poetry of Earth and Sea* by Athénaïs Mialaret Michelet, but have been altered for the purposes of this story.

Cover photo by Zoharby

Printed in the U.S.A.

Table of Contents

Glacier Des Bossons

Glacier de Tacconaz

Chamonix-Mont Blanc Region (Not to Scale)

Rochers Rouge on Left. Grand Plateau on Right (Not to Scale)

Snow Crystal, magnified, courtesy Wikicommons

Example natural Ice Crystal, courtesy
Wikicommons

Front of Letter Written By John Auldjo atop Mont Blanc, source: Alpine Club

Back of Letter Written By John Auldjo atop Mont Blanc, signed by guides, source: Alpine Club

CLIMBING TERMINOLOGY

Arête
A small ridge-like feature or a sharp outward facing corner on a steep rock face

Col
A small pass or "saddle" between two peaks.

Crampons
Metal framework with spikes attached to boots to increase safety on snow and ice.

Glissade
A usually voluntary act of sliding down a steep slope of snow.

Glacier
A slow moving mass of ice formed by the accumulation and compaction of snow on mountains

Ice Cliff
A wall of ice that can be severely overhung and unstable and is formed by a glacier high on a mountain side flowing over a rock cliff.

Wind Slab
A type of snow crust; a patch of hard-packed snow, which is packed as it is deposited.

INDEX OF CHARACTERS

Jon Miller – free-lance writer, narrator of story
Ana Miller –wife of Jon, co-writer
Sean Miller – deceased son of Jon and Ana

Stan –editor-in-chief at *The Climb*

Horace-Bénédict de Saussure – Geneva aristocrat, physicist and Alpine traveler, often considered the founder of alpinism, and considered to be the first person to build a successful solar oven.

Jacques Balmat – nicknamed "Mont Blanc" was a mountaineer and mountain guide, born in the Chamonix valley of the Savoy region, and the first man to summit Mont Blanc.

Three Chamonix Guides who first attempted ascent – Francois Paccard, Joseph Carrier, and Jean-Michel Fournier

Dr. Michel Gabriel Paccard – doctor and alpinist, Born in Chamonix, studied medicine in Turin. Due to his passion for botany and minerals, he met Horace-Bénédict de Saussure, who initiated the race to be the first to ascend Mont Blanc. He ascended Mont Blanc with Jacques Balmat.

The Chamonix Guides (all male) –
Pierre Balmat, died on the mountain in 1820
Pierre Carrier, died on the mountain in 1820
Auguste Tairray, died on the mountain in 1820

Joseph-Marie (JM) Coutet, nearly killed in the 1820 attempt

Simeon Devouassoux

Jean-Pierre Tairraz

Julien Devouassoux

Pierre-Joseph Simond

Simon Tournier

Michel Devouassoux

Pierre Simon

Mathieu Balmat

Jacques Simond

Michel Favret

Jean-Marie Coutet

Auguste Couttet, a guide's apprentice

Michel Carrier, attempted to find the body of Jacques Balmat

Auguste Balmat, great nephew of Jacques Balmat

Dr. Hamel – Russian physicist who attempted to climb Mont Blanc to test a scientific apparatus at high altitude. Several members of his party were killed in their ascent of 1820. Young Dornford and Henderson were part of the surviving members.

Maria Paradis – a poor maid, first woman to summit Mont Blanc 1808. From then on, she was nicknamed "Maria de Mont Blanc"

Favret – an old guide and whose hut was the last inhabited spot on the mountain, 19th century

Dr. Edmund Clark and **Captain Markham Sherwill** ascended the summit in 1825.

Monsieur Simon – Advisor to Dr. Clark.
Madame Simond – Inn keeper where Dr. Clark stayed.

Coutet le Chamois – old porter
John Auldjo – traveler, geologist, writer, Deputy Grand Master of Upper Canada and later, British Consul at Geneva, ascended in 1827.

Martin Barry –British physician who studied histology and embryology, ascended in 1834.

Paul Verne – brother of author Jules Verne is believed to be the fortieth ascent of Mont Blanc.
Edward & Ambroise Ravanal, Gaspar Simond – guides to Paul Verne.
Levesque – Climbing companion of Paul Verne.

The Mountain

It had happened again. On July 12, 2012, nine climbers were killed by avalanches as they attempted a dawn ascent of Mont Maudit, the 14,649 foot mountain that makes up part of the Mont Blanc mountain range. Several others were injured and four went missing.

As a freelance writer, I was haltingly asked by Stan, the editor-in-chief at *The Climb*, a quarterly journal, to travel to the region to write about those who dared to ascend Mont Blanc. He was reluctant to call me because eleven months ago, our twenty-two year old son, Sean, had died. While out partying with friends, he tripped on an uneven sidewalk and hit his head, never to awaken again. It seems ludicrous, but it is all too real.

Stan was surprised I accepted the assignment. My wife, Ana, and I are eager for a change of scenery. Every reminder of Sean is too real; too overwhelming. The sadness is worse than the shock and the shock is worse than any physical pain. In the enormity of it, Ana and I alternate in drifting apart and then in turn, cling to each other. Blame, fear, guilt and grief dominate our days. In some queer sense, there is comfort in knowing that nothing – nothing – could hurt more than this.

I was twenty and Ana was nineteen when Sean was born. Children raising children can be a difficult thing and we are tortured by age-old regrets and haunting what-ifs now that he is gone.

In mid-August 2012, we left California for Chamonix, France, the lofty village at the base of Mont Blanc and the site of the first Winter Olympics in 1924. I did basic research of the region before we left and what I discovered was its grand allure brought infinite numbers of tourists, admirers and of course, climbers. See, men and women don't come to Mont Blanc to conquer the mountain. They come here because they have already been conquered by all it promises.

Do not be fooled. This mass is not a lump, a wart, *a thing*. Rather, this mountain is a living, respirating being whose very existence beckons, tempts, teases and whose charms cannot be shaken. Its lovers have willingly flung themselves off the jagged cliffs. Were they of right mind or had the mountain cast a spell upon them? I am here to find out. I have since conceived that Mont Blanc and its conspiratorial cousins may not take your life, but it will take something.

Since receiving the assignment, the mystery of White Mountain has tugged at both of us. Ana is eager to explore this grand aspect of Nature and we take up this journey of exploration together. I can't travel and write and be away from her for long periods and expect our marriage to endure, particularly during this time of crises. Our daily togetherness, working and living, has its pressures, but less threat than being apart. She is walled off by grief and we have not been intimate since just before Sean's death. Perhaps we both feel too guilty to enjoy ourselves. Living on his own, working and thriving, there was not much we could have done to prevent our son's death, but guilt is not necessarily a rational emotion.

Ana is too tender to be sarcastic, but we have our conflict outside of this shared grief. Over the years, she has expressed with deep frustration that our life is really *my* life and that she follows without much choice. She further endures the stress of me pursuing projects that she is largely against due to the time and effort it takes with little compensation. She calls my writing style, "without warmth and analytical." She seeks to encourage me in the direction of free and lofty prose much like her own. I have always worked alone and she has been left to find her own path. Now that we are here together, her influence upon me is felt in our confined quarters as her well of suppressed creativity bubbles to the surface.

She made it clear that if she was not going to participate in this project in some meaningful way, she was not about to join me on this trip. If I pursue my work alone, I lose my marriage of twenty-three years. Loss upon loss is a burden I know I am too weak to carry at this time. I would rather attempt to collaborate as writers than face that outcome. The long mournful months spent in bed sobbing have done nothing but encourage more of the same. Therefore, we are here to blend together our talents and find a reason to live again. I was delighted to see Ana enter eagerly into this and I think decisively because I believe she has been destined since childhood to write down her keen observations of Nature.

When we arrived at Sallenches, we were struck by the starkness of the scene. It was a gloomy day, which is typical for the greater part of the year in this region. I was able to see Mont Blanc in its reality, its meanness and its poverty; towering there like an ice cold giant. It does not offer on its mid-slope those great highways of the nations by which France, Germany and Italy are eternally crossing. It stands apart. You would have to go expressly to see and salute the illustrious hermit whose head dominates Europe.

In my travel for work, I had already seen the Apennines, the Pyrenees; the great hospitable mountains of the merchant and the traveler (Mont Cenis and Saint Gothard) as well as the swift magic of the Simplon Pass. I preferred the giant hermit even before our arrival. I told myself its elusive peak of 15,781 feet was its grand allure, but I soon learned it was much more than that.

Behind the cold decoration of winter, there lies concealed a being we do not see. The ices (some 1,200 feet in thickness) are for it a simple garb. This being made of granite is buried within its tomb of snow. The soul of the mountain remains in close affinity with its profound mother, Earth, and it thrives beneath her genial expansion.

The surrounding water is cold, the wind icy; yet all around, there are hot springs. How our limbs, aching from the travel, yearned to sink beneath the warm waters. For that pleasure, we would almost die for it. Those ancient pools of fire that lavishly pour out their burning waters are common in this region. Here, beneath this immense shroud of ice and snow, their existence provokes the thought that Nature always seeks to maintain harmony and balance.

In the village of Saint Gervais, the whole scene seemed to greet us with fun and laughter. I found its beauty touching and it went straight to my heart. The rain began falling, but we experienced a certain quickening of the spirit. Life seems fresh here. Was this the effect of the air (at a mere altitude of 2,400 feet)? Would the entire world be relieved of its burdens if it was able to profit from this mountain air?

I don't know if Chamonix is calculated to soothe the heart, but it does. When we arrived, it seemed haunted by friendly spirits, even in the pouring rain. It is closely shut in; ensnaring all of its inhabitants, but a deep relaxation filled us. On either side, the fir trees overhang and cast strange shadows. Long dragon-like trains of fog are attracted from the river Arve. The whole area seems replete with mysteries, dreams and illusions. I could only wish for more light in the ravines as they seem the darkest and coldest of places.

The months best suited for alpine climbing had now passed, so the valley is less populated. Ana and I are not staying at the entrance overlooking the course of the Arve, but at the other end of the village in a little house situated on somewhat lower ground. We are living a little haphazard with finances being tight. Though our pockets are threadbare, we find our souls richly rewarded in these surroundings.

As soon as the rain ceased, we set out on an exploring journey. All the landscape was still exceedingly dank. Under the venerable walnut trees, the road was very muddy and the sky sprinkled with drops of rain. It was market day. The village was full of animation; shoppers bustled about the stalls.

The weather was unable to decide between the sun and the rain. On the hillside, the rams seemed delighted in the inclement weather. Little streams sang and babbled, but the sky darkened more and the snow, by degrees, assumed the dull hue of lead. We returned home.

Ana re-entered our abode in a serious mood, but with hands full of flowers. She seems to have been affected by the change in the sky. She placed the flowers in a vase and stroked them at intervals throughout the night. She is quiet and thoughtful and I dare not intrude upon her thoughts because I know where they lie; on a dark-haired boy now lost to us.

At times, it is painful to look at my wife as Sean's features are distinctly recognizable in her face. They share the round face, dark hair and blue eyes that have nothing to do with me. My thinning, pale blonde hair, brown eyes and oversized nose on a long face did not show up in our son. Each year, the furrows on my brow deepen and seem to add another crease, like rungs on a ladder. I often wonder what Sean would look like as a grown man.

He did, however, have my baritone voice and my fingers, long and knotty; and he typed in the same manner, like a horse prancing, as he toyed with following in my footsteps to become a sports writer. Crazy for extreme sports, a keen skateboarder, surfer and bike rider, we never considered that a stupid uneven sidewalk would be his end.

So here we are in Chamonix, brought here by death to forget our son's death. What a messed-up thought – as if we could ever "get over it." But we have to plow on through this thing called grief.

The next morning was light; a little cold, but agreeable and lively. Ana was smiling and her manner was playful. Together, we wrote of our observations thus far. Snow powdered the lofty hills and it was an inspiring scene to see from the window by the desk where our papers, thoughts and ideas weighed. We took a break to visit our neighbors, the fir trees of the cataract. We studied those venerable resinous patriarchs; the eldest-born of the world. In the more difficult ages, they endured many hardships and today still support and defend exposed localities. They seem to be the natural brothers of all suffering and laborious populations.

The forest of firs appeared on the right shoulder of the hill. We ventured on and crossed the Devil's Bridge (a commonly used name for bridges throughout Europe). The fir-wood was exceedingly beautiful here. It presented a succession of somber avenues with a fantastic effect that alternately concealed and displayed the windings of the valley below. In their black antiquity, the firs rendered the forest darker and more obscure.

On emerging and climbing towards a more open spot, we saw the whole valley and the road to the glaciers. It was an extensive, tranquil scene contrasted with a very human view as there in the hollow, human toil was evident.

The entire scene was rendered solemn and affecting by the presage of a storm, but we were not eager to leave. Strangely, the human soul takes comfort in impending doom. We sat on a narrow ridge of stone and remained silent. We are too much alike in our thoughts to have to speak.

The rain was still on its way. In a month or two, it would feel like winter. All was soft and calm. The mutability of everything painfully affected me. I felt a great want within me, but the imposing bulk of the mountain promised me nothing.

Temptation

Long before visiting Mont Blanc, I had seen the Grindelwald glacier in Switzerland. It is an easily accessible glacier whose approaches are not denuded of all their natural character like those of too many other glaciers where artificial effects have been carefully prepared.

That morning, so many years ago, I left noisy Interlaken with its vulgar affluence and arrived at the village. I took a room at Grindelwald in a simple hotel. The dim chamber was nothing remarkable, but when the attendant opened a window, I was startled. The casement was overflowing with an indefinable, radiant, moving light as if something otherworldly was advancing towards me. In that moment, nothing seemed more formidable. It was luminous chaos. All fell to the wayside; it was just me and the light. The effect could not have been grander if a star had suddenly touched Earth. I was enthralled and captivated and transported to a Heaven I have only imagined.

When I recovered from the enchanting light, I approached the window and saw the glacier in all the force of its astonishment and horror. It had the appearance of being in motion. It now halted and appeared to rest at my feet in profound depth. Though motionless, the glacier now seemed again to be moving, as if it was trying to sneak up on me! Its whole surface was encrusted with sugar-loaf crystals of little brilliancy from fifteen to twenty feet in height. Some were of a whitish color, a few shaded with pale blue, others of a bottle-green tint, equivocal and sinister.

All this, lit up by the sun, wore an aspect of savage harshness; a grand effect of superb indifference to us mortals. From my research, I recalled that when famous alpine explorer Horace-Bénédict de Saussure ascended the glacier, he said an emotion of anger overtook him. Gazing over at it, I too felt myself surprised and incensed by the wild enormity of it. Here, man is revealed as small. Little did I know then that a decade later, I would feel even smaller; diminished by a grief so crushing, I felt that I barely existed.

I left the village and went to explore the Lower Grindelwald Glacier. I touched upon its border and entered its grandeur. The glacier gaped with a narrow mouth, shining and polished. Everywhere there were mysterious and dangerous declivities. The slopes, with their sharp fractures, sharp even to the eye, warned me not to trust them. I could not help but smile upon seeing a charming posy of flowers embedded in the ice still with all its living colors. Once swallowed up, all is well-preserved. No image of death can be more impressive than this long glassed-in exhibition and the impossibility of returning to an animated nature.

In the early nineteenth century, the local mountaineer did not regard this glacier from the same viewpoint as us. He was strongly attached to it and constantly returned to it, but he still called it "the evil mountain." The white glassy waters that escape from it, leaping and bounding in furious rapidity, he named "the wild waters" because they often threatened to wash away his modest home. The black forest, on the precipice, was his battlement at one time of the year and then his war in the roughest months of the year.

When all other labor ceased, he attacked the forest for survival. It was an arduous campaign and full of perils. It was not enough to chop down the trees. Their course had to be directed. He had to watch them on their passage and regulate the terrible obstacles that impeded its path as it made its way along the wild water. The forest has its mournful history of orphans and widows as the woodsmen lost their lives guiding the journey of the felled tree.

At one time, the glaciers were objects of aversion. The Germans of Switzerland sentenced the damned to the glaciers. If you think about it, they are a kind of hell if you are caught alone and without proper equipment. A Scandinavian legend gives fantastical expression to the terrors of the glacier. It says they are stored with tempting treasures that are guarded by frightful gnomes and a dwarf of colossal strength.

The tale says that inside the castle sits enthroned a pitiless virgin with a diamond-blazing forehead. She incenses every mountain hero. Her laugh is sharper than the keen shafts of a winter gale. Yet, the heedless still dash onward. When they reach their fatal bed, they remain enchained, celebrating eternal nuptials with the virgin bride of crystal. However, this does not discourage the climber. The cruel and haughty virgin teases her would-be lovers and as if mindlessly, they follow her beckon. They yearn for her, travel for thousands of miles to ascend to her, without understanding they are her prey.

In my laborious assessment of the glaciers, I accomplished more ascents and descended more precipices seated at the table where I write than all the climbers on Earth. But I was wrong to think the crystallized palaces were the attraction to the climber. The allure of the mountain is much more powerful than that.

Avalanche

It is in the much lower elevations of Mont Blanc's range where Ana and I have agreed to limit our climbs. There is no reason to take on mortal risk during a time when we are perhaps the least interested in preserving our lives. In our state of grief, we can relate to the profound sense of loss felt by the survivors of those who died while attempting to ascend the mountain that July of 2012. Chamonix is filled with conversations and stories about that deadly day.

Like most mountain disasters, the actual events will never be fully known, as they are so often colored by the perspective and imagination of others.

That awful sound, the hiss and crack and fall of massive amounts of ice and snow, is not one we can ever get used to. Each time we hear that roar, we cringe, hoping no one is in its devouring path.

The tragedy of July 12, 2012 struck just after five in the morning. The climbing party began an ascent of Mont Maudit in that early dawn light to perhaps reach the summit at a decent hour. It is believed the climbers were roped together in at least two teams. In doing so, their fate was also tethered to each other. No less dangerous than its great cousin, Mont Maudit is called the Accursed Mountain for a reason.

According to footage taken of the disaster, and based on the accounts of first responders, an ice cliff had fallen off the mountain and triggered the avalanche.

Appallingly, the mountain rescuers searched the entire avalanche area, but could not find the missing climbers. Conditions were difficult and dangerous. One of the rescuers believed the avalanche took place in two phases; the initial serac, approximately 250 meters wide, had hit the climbers who were higher up on the Maudit face. The second slide was believed to be due to a wind slab that swept away the climbers further down.

Wind slabs are one of the most dangerous aspects of the mountains in the summer months because the ice is melting. With a massive slab rushing headlong into climbers, there is not much that can be done to prevent disaster. Only staying off the mountain could have saved lives, but the climber is here to climb.

There were many who said the conditions were not remotely favorable for such a climb and that the party was either ill-advised or careless, but others argued there was no weather bulletin issued to warn of such an event. Later, officials said heavy snowfall and high winds had created the perfect conditions for an avalanche around Mont Blanc. The dead included three British, one Swiss, three Germans and two Spanish climbers.

"In the front, there were really experienced mountain guides. It was a tragic accident. I think those people, they were at the wrong place at the wrong time," said mountain guide, Klemen Gričar. "I saw a French guide with a dislocated shoulder, badly injured, shaking because of strong wind and cold, so it was really horrible."

While many in the group of twenty-eight mountaineers escaped the avalanche, nine people were treated at a local hospital for minor injuries.

Euronews correspondent, Alberto de Filippis, said: "The normal route to Mont Blanc from the refuge known as the 'Cosmic Hut' is not particularly difficult. It is a path used every year by hundreds of tourists and does not require special technical skills. For most climbers, the real challenge would have begun a day later when they attempted a further 1,000 meter climb to Mont Maudit. It was there the mountain gave way and took with it at least nine lives."

Those who survived the Mont Maudit avalanche were lucky. It was not as if the mountain had not given ample prior warnings.

In August 1985, two Spanish climbers died in an avalanche.

An avalanche in August of 1993 took the lives of eight climbers on the Mont Blanc massif.

In July of 1994, nine people succumbed in an avalanche.

Three Germans and one Israeli died in an avalanche in July 1996.

Twelve people perished and a significant portion of the village of Montrox, at the foot of the Mont Blanc massif, was destroyed by an avalanche in February 1999.

In August of 2000, three Germans and two French mountaineers were killed in an avalanche on the Tour Ronde peak.

A French climber and his guide were killed while descending Mont Blanc du Tacul in July of 2004.

A British soldier was killed in July 2005 when an avalanche struck during a training expedition. His group of six was in the midst of descending the peak of Mont Blanc du Tacul when the slide was triggered.

In June of 2007, a female hiker was killed in an avalanche on Mont Blanc du Tacul.

Three Polish climbers were found dead on Mont Blanc after an avalanche in July 2007.

Five Austrian and three Swiss climbers died on Mont Blanc du Tacul in August of 2008.

After mercifully sparing the lives of climbers for a few years, the mountain had now struck again.

Two survivors, French and Danish climbers, spoke to the European media from their hospital beds shortly after the accident.

"We felt the snow but we could still resist it – but then big chunks of snow fell onto us and then we were swept away. We all fell together and that's it. It all happened so quickly. We were happy when it started to slow down," said French Guide Daniel Rossetto.

The Danish survivor said: "I was climbing up with the ice axes and all of a sudden, big pieces of ice fell down right next to us. And I thought, 'That would have really hurt if those had hit us'. Then a split second after that, it all came down and hit us and blew us away."

Rescue efforts were strong and determined to find those who had perished or those who were missing, but it was difficult. As the French interior minister somberly stated, "The Mountain doesn't always give up its victims."

Attraction

So why do people come here? The reality is that the climber mounts for the sake of mounting. Once the thrill of the climb gets under your skin, there is no turning back. Even in the face of near death, you return; though perhaps to a lower elevation.

There is actually very little profit in the ascent of Mont Blanc. Years ago, the experiments made on its summit could probably have been made at a lower level. Yet, all want to ascend to the summit to declare they have achieved such a lofty goal. Of course, that is the whole purpose of being there. People boldly confront the ice, fog, abysses, crevasses, the deceitful distance, the falsities of perspective and the unbridled whirl of vertigo. These only act as a greater stimulus. Men and women, in all other areas mostly sage and prudent, here go mad. The raptures of love for the climb might be compared to the awful delight of pursuing a prey into the abyss.

There is an age-old story of a father and son climbing the mountain. The father, wild and crazed with an evil grin willingly jumped to his death. The son returned a year later after declaring to his weeping new bride, "As my father perished, I too must perish." The son kept his word by flinging himself off the same precipice.

In the nineteenth century, many eagerly gathered in groups to listen to the hunter or the climber as they related like oracles their ascents. Even today, a whole crowd seems to tremble when the storyteller describes gazing into the ominous azure of a yawning crevasse. He or she describes vaults of twenty, thirty or one hundred feet in height. Grottoes are all sparkling with crystals or maybe even diamonds. How many people would perish if they were in fact diamonds? For those who could survive the climb, what evil would there be in robbing the devil that is Mont Blanc?

Early on, Chamonix-Mont Blanc was largely ignored. The traveler did not make his way along the lower ground through that long and gloomy valley. Rather, it was the passing wayfarer who, as he followed the route of Notre Dame de la Gorge (the road to Italy), saw the snowy mass of Mont Blanc.

From a close viewpoint, you can see it in all its loftiness; an immense white monk buried in its cloak and hood of ice. It seems dead and yet standing erect. Others see in it a splendor like the ruins of a dying star, a pale and barren moon or a sepulchral upon a terrestrial planet. Its vast snowy hood has the effect of a cemetery whose monuments are the somber pyramids that start up in striking contrast with the snow. If the traveler goes to the mountain base, he finds himself in a ravine, impassable and gloomy for eight months of the year. The valley is imprisoned in it. Under the foot of the colossus, it is difficult to breathe.

How much more at ease I was on Mont Cenis or the Saint Gothard. Their summits, solemn as they may be, are the natural highways of all animated life. What numbers of horses and migratory birds there were. In contrast, Mont Blanc leads nowhere; it is a hermit wrapped up in its solitary musings.

There is a strange enigma Ana and I discovered in the Alps. While every other peak is eloquent with the voices of innumerable streams, Mont Blanc, the great miser, grudgingly yields two tiny torrents that enlarge as they are enriched by other waters. It receives a lot, yet it gives very little. Does it have a subterranean treasure trove of water? Is this giant hermit prudently amassing water as a precaution against the future thirst and drought of the globe?

In 1762, the first attempt to reach the summit was made by Pierre Simon of Chamonix, who endeavored to accomplish it by the Glacier des Bossons and again from the French side, but failed in both. As early as 1767, numerous grottoes were discovered that had been excavated and rifled by the crystal hunters. Another unsuccessful attempt was made by four villagers in 1775. After triumphing over the obstacles that opposed their way, the four guides penetrated into a great valley of snow that seemed as if it would reach Mont Blanc. The weather was favorable, they met with no appalling precipices or yawning crevasses and all things apparently promised success; but the rarefaction of the air and the reverberation of the sun's rays on the dazzling surface wearied them beyond endurance. Succumbing to physical and mental fatigue, they gave up their attempt.

Seven years later, in 1783, three guides of the village, Francois Paccard, Joseph Carrier and Jean-Michel Fournier, attempted the ascent, but they also failed. The deadly lethargy overtook one of them and compelled the others to carry their comrade back to Chamonix.

Back in the village, one of the guides told Horace-Bénédict de Saussure, a man of sagacious intellect who was determined to ascend Mont Blanc, that it was perfectly useless to carry provisions in making the ascent because it was impossible to eat; and that if he ever tried it again, the only things he would carry would be a light parasol and a bottle of scent.

"When I pictured to myself," said de Saussure, "this strong and robust mountaineer climbing these mountains of snow, in one hand holding a parasol and in the other a bottle of perfume, it presented so strange and ridiculous an image that nothing could give me a better idea of the difficulty of the enterprise, and of the absolute impossibility of any man, who had not the head and legs of a Chamonix guide, ever to accomplish it."

In 1784, a guide was fortunate enough to chance upon a great quantity of crystals and brought away three hundred pounds of large translucent crystals of a beautiful purple hue. This event turned the brains of the mountaineers. One of the Balmats (a celebrated family of guides renowned for their foremost intrepidity) ascended, but found nothing. A terrible tempest challenged him and put his life at great peril. The spirits of the mountain doubtlessly sought to discourage the rash and heedless treasure hunters.

That same year, a naturalist attained a point so near the summit that he resolved to renew the enterprise in 1785. Horace-Bénédict de Saussure accompanied him. They set out at eight in the morning on September 12, 1785; bivouacked at the base of the Aiguille du Goûter and on the following day reached an elevation of 11,250 feet. Due to foul weather, they were forced to abandon their attempt.

Of the belief that the obstacles were the result only of the advanced season, de Saussure determined to follow up his enterprise by the same route. He hired Pierre Balmat to build a stone cabin on one of the shelves of the Aiguille to be ready for the attempt and to chart the state of the snow.

In the execution of this project, Pierre Balmat and two other guides climbed up the Aiguille on June 8, 1786 and reached the top of the Dôme du Goûter with great toil and pain; suffering acutely from the rarefaction of the air. Here, they fell in with Francois Paccard and three other guides who had ascended by the ridge of the mountain that divides the lower part of the Glacier des Bossons from that of Taconnaz.

This rendezvous had been agreed upon so they could determine which route was the most advantageous. The preference was given to Dôme du Goûter. Uniting their forces, they traversed a large plain of snow and gained a huge ridge which connected the top of Mont Blanc with the Dôme du Goûter. However, this was so steep and narrow that its passage was impossible. They investigated every portion of the plain and coming to the conclusion that, as far as this route was concerned, the summit of Mont Blanc appeared more inaccessible than ever. They sulkily returned to Chamonix harassed by a fearful storm of snow and hail in which they were nearly lost.

It just so happened that one of Paccard's party, a man named Jacques Balmat (who apparently was not very popular in the valley) had presented himself without invitation on the excursion and followed them against their will.

Francois Paccard, a native of Chamonix, had some suspicion that Jacques Balmat knew a track they could follow with some prospect of success, and tried to get details out of Balmat.

Balmat refused to reveal any information.

The Prize

With modern climbing equipment and clothing, it can be hard to imagine what it was like for those early mountain explorers. Despite hardship, they were not deterred and remained competitive to summit Mont Blanc.

Horace-Bénédict de Saussure offered a reward for the first man to ascend the mountain. The intrepid and tenacious Jacques Balmat was obsessed with claiming the prize. The account of his quest to summit Mont Blanc is best outlined in his journal, as follows:

Ascent of Jacques Balmat

"The determination to reach the summit of Mont Blanc was jogging in my brain night and day. During the day, I would ascend the Brevent, where I passed hours trying to see a way to my coveted summit. I felt that I would live in a sort of purgatory if I did not succeed.

At night, I had hardly closed my eyes when I dreamed I was on my climb of discovery. I fixed my nails into the rock so they may act like cramps. I reached out, trying to clasp a branch. I raised myself up by my knees like a chimney sweep. The branch was in reach. I clutched at it! Suddenly, my wife awoke me with a great slap. I was grasping at her, not a branch.

I got out of bed and got dressed.

"Where are you going?" she demanded.

"To sleep on the mountain!"

I took a strong stock with good iron points double the length and thickness of an ordinary one. I filled a gourd with water and put a morsel of bread in my pocket and away I went.

I had repeatedly tried to ascend by the Mer de Glace, but Mont Maudit had always barred my way. I returned by way of the Aiguille du Goûter, but to ascend to the Dôme du Goûter there is a backbone of rock a quarter of a league long, two feet wide and below, a depth of 1,800 feet. This time, I was resolved to try another route.

I began the route that ultimately leads to the mountain of La Côte and after three hours ascent, I reached the Glacier des Bossons and I crossed it. It was not difficult. Four hours later, I was at the Grands Mulets. That gave me something to celebrate so I ate a crust of bread and drank a cup of water.

At the end of two and a half hours of research, I found a place bare of snow, about six or seven feet. There, I installed myself on the rock where I was going to pass the night. I broke off a second crust and drank my second cup. It did not take me long to make my bed.

At approximately nine, I saw a shadow rise from the valley like thick smoke. It advanced slowly towards me. It reached and enveloped me. Notwithstanding this shroud, I could see above me the last reflected rays of the setting sun which seemed loath to leave the highest point of Mont Blanc. But the rays did disappear and with them, the day.

On my left side was the immense plain of snow that reaches to the Dôme du Goûter and on my right, a precipice 800 feet deep. I dared not go to sleep for fear of falling off the edge while dreaming. Instead, I sat on my bag and stamped my feet and clapped my hands incessantly to keep up the circulation.

Soon, the moon rose. It was pale and veiled in a circle of clouds. At eleven, I saw a nasty mist cloud coming from the Aiguille du Goûter. As soon as it reached me, it smacked me in the face with a dash of snow.

"Keep moving!" I yelled at it.

I heard the fall of avalanches rolling down with a horrible rumbling sound like thunder. The glaciers cracked and with every crack, the mountain shook under me. Neither hungry nor thirsty, I experienced a singular kind of headache. The pain began at the crown of my head and worked its way down my face. The mist-fog continued. My breath became congealed on my handkerchief. The snow, having penetrated through my clothes, made me feel naked. I redoubled my movements and compelled myself to sing in order to drive away a heap of horrible thoughts that began to haunt my mind. This mountain wanted my soul and I was not giving it to her! But my voice was lost in the snow. No echo answered to it. All was death-like in the midst of this frozen Nature. I was abysmally alone. The sound of my voice had a strange effect on me. I became afraid that I would commit suicide. A man has a lot to think about when alone and without the distraction of toys or other humans.

Some part of me was aware that my thoughts could uplift or destroy me. I am the master of my thoughts, the builder of my character and the one who would shape my destiny. I was the one who held the key to this accomplishment if I could remain sharp of mind and mindful of thoughts that were out to destroy me. I could easily die out here alone. It would only require the simple closing of my eyes. Is that not the universal preference for death; to leave this world by way of eternal slumber? Yet, I loved this mountain too much. I wanted to live, if only for it.

At last, at two, the sky began to whiten towards the east. I felt my courage returning as the sun rose and battled the clouds shrouding Mont Blanc. I trusted Father Sun would chase them away, but by four, they became denser. With the effects of the sun becoming feebler as the day progressed, I came to the conclusion that it would be impossible to ascend further that day.

In order not to waste such an opportunity, I instead explored the neighboring glaciers and passed the whole day in reconnoitering the best passages. As evening advanced and the mists followed, I descended to the Bec-de-la-Oiseau (Beak of the Bird) where night overtook me. I passed this night better than the last, but when I awoke, I was frozen through and through. It was only when I reached the village of Moud that my clothes began to thaw.

I had gone about a hundred steps past the last houses in this village when I met three guides, Francois Paccard, Joseph Carrier, and Jean-Michel Fournier, a tight-knit group of friends similar in character and disposition (in other words, I trusted none of them). They had their bags and batons and wore their climbing gear. I asked them where they were headed. They replied that they were in search of some goats, but this silly answer made me think they were trying to deceive me. I felt convinced they were going to attempt the ascent which I had just failed and consequently, they would claim the reward de Saussure had promised to the first one to reach the summit.

One or two questions the guide Paccard put to me about different points and whether one could sleep at the Bec-de-la-Oiseau confirmed my suspicions. I replied that it was covered with snow and that as a resting station, it appeared to me to be an inadvisable spot. He exchanged a sign with the others that I pretended not to notice. They consulted together and ended by proposing that we should all ascend together. I accepted, but having promised my wife that I would not stay away more than three days, I went home to tell her.

I changed my gear and collected some provisions as my wife followed me from room to room begging me not to leave. Her words fell on deaf ears as I could only hear the call of the mountain.

At eleven at night, I started out again without having been to bed. By one in the morning, I rejoined my comrades at the Bec-de-la-Oiseau. They were all sleeping like marmots. I noisily awakened them and they were all rapidly on their feet. The four of us set forward on our journey. We crossed the glacier of Tacconnaz and ascended as far as the Grands Mulets where two nights before I had passed such hideous hours. Taking a course to the right at about three o'clock, we reached the Dôme du Goûter. Paccard was short of breath. A little above the Grands Mulets he laid down, covered with the coat of one of his comrades.

Arriving at last at the top of the Dôme, we saw something black moving on the Aiguille du Goûter. We could not distinguish what it was. It turned out to be newcomers wanting to join our climbing party. It was Pierre Balmat and a friend who had made a bet with the others that they would reach the Dôme du Goûter before us. Well, they had lost that bet.

I was becoming annoyed with the whole group and I left them to clear my head and to examine the arête (a sharp narrow ridge). I climbed towards the arête and got a quarter of a league nearer to the animal. I believe I could have succeeded in reaching the end had it not been cut in two with crevasses. In addition, the arête was so sharp I could not walk upon it. Not wanting to have to return backwards and astride, I retraced my way back to where I had left my fellow climbers. They were all gone; just my knapsack sat there alone.

I felt abandoned and upset. For an instant, I was suspended between the wish to join them and the desire to attempt the ascent by myself, but then who would be there to witness my success? Their desertion piqued me. Something ferocious told me that I would succeed this time. I took up my bag and once more set off.

It was now four in the afternoon. I crossed the Grand Plateau as far as the Brevent. I could see the valleys in Piedmont. Mist was on the summit of Mont Blanc. I did not attempt to ascend; less from a fear that I would die than from a feeling of certainty that the others would never believe that I had reached the summit alone.

I took advantage of what remained of the day to seek shelter and spent an hour in vain doing so. As I recalled that one awful night plagued by thoughts, I resolved to return home. I commenced my descent, but when I arrived at the Grand Plateau, not having provided myself with protective eye gear, the snow had so fatigued my eyes that I could see nothing. I had a kind of dazzling giddiness that caused me only to envision great drops of blood.

I sat down in order to restore myself. I let my head fall between my hands. At the end of half an hour, my sight came back, but the night had come with it. I had no time to lose. I arose to go, but had scarcely taken a hundred steps when I felt with my baton that there was no depth of ice under my feet. I was on the edge of a great crevasse where three guides had perished some time ago.

In the morning, it had been a bridge of ice covered with snow. This I tried to find, but the night was growing darker and my sight worse. I could not find it. The pain in my head again attacked me. I felt no desire to eat or drink; violent palpitations of the heart made me almost vomit. I had to make up my mind to remain close to the crevasse until daybreak because to find the bridge of ice would take me at least another hour. I put down my bag on the snow and made a curtain of my handkerchief. I did my best to prepare for the night, but having experienced it awfully the night before, I felt intense dread.

Being 12,000 feet high, there is a much more intense cold. A fine needle-like snow froze me. I felt a languor and an irresistible desire to sleep. The most sad and awful thoughts came across my mind. I thought of how poorly I had treated my wife, the neighborhood dogs and my brothers. I cringed upon thinking what I had become in pursuit of this peak. I told myself that once I did ascend to the summit, it would release me from its grip.

I knew the gloomy ideas and longing for sleep were bad signs. If I had the misfortune to close my eyes, I would never open them again. I could see the lights of Chamonix and imagined my comrades were warming themselves by their firesides or were comfortably in bed. Perhaps not one of them had given me a thought. Or, if one did think of me, perhaps he wished me to keep up my courage.

It was not courage that I wanted now, but strength. I'm not made of iron and I felt that I was ill. In the short intervals of silence between the momentary falls of avalanches and the cracking of the glacier, I heard the barking of a dog down in the village. Was it the dog I had kicked out of my way when I headed out that day? The poor hound was reminding me of what I had done. This took my thoughts away from myself and I thought of all those down in the village below me.

About two, I saw the white line of dawn on the horizon. The sun followed. Mont Blanc had put on his white wig and when he does that, he is in a bad mood. I know his character well. As we say in the valley, "When he smokes his pipe, one must not try to put it out."

When daybreak came, I was frozen. By practicing the most absurd gymnastics, my limbs became supple and I was able to begin exploring once more.

I had observed, when descending to the Grand Plateau, that half-way down there was a steep incline leading straight to the top of the Rochers Rouges. I decided to scale it, but found it too steep. The snow was so hard that I could only hold on by making holes with the iron point of my stock. I succeeded in clinging to it, but I felt extreme fatigue. It was not an amusing thing to be suspended by one leg over an abyss and be obliged to cut the ice with an already blunt point. By force of patience and perseverance, I gained and said out loud, "From this spot to the summit, there's nothing more to hinder me!"

But I was again frozen through and through, and almost dead with hunger and thirst.

It was late. *I must descend. I will succeed next time in better weather.*

When I reached home, I was almost blind. When my sight became somewhat restored, I went to lie down in the basement and there, I slept for 48 hours without waking.

Three weeks elapsed without bringing any favorable change in the weather and without diminishing my ardor to make a third attempt. I imparted the secret of my discovery to the village doctor, Dr. Michel Paccard, and discussed with him my future intentions. We agreed we would go together the first fine day.

A fine gentleman was Paccard, although a bit timid and unsure of himself. I selected him as a climbing companion for his doctor skills and for the fact that he would not try to summit the mountain before me. As long as he was going to be second on the peak, I was happy with his companionship.

On August 8, 1786, the weather appeared sufficiently settled to hazard another trial. I went to Paccard and said to him, "Now, Doctor, are you up to it? Have you any fear of snow, ice or precipices? Speak out like a man."

"I have fear of nothing when I am with you, Balmat!"

"Well, then," I said, "the moment has come."

Paccard said he was quite ready, but when he shut his door, I think his courage began to fail him. His key would not leave the lock.

"Why don't we stay, Balmat?" he said. "We really should take two guides with us."

"No," I replied, "I ascend with you alone or you ascend with others. I want to be the first, not the second."

He reflected for a moment, drew out the key and then slowly put it into his pocket. He followed me mechanically with his head lowered. In an instant, his confidence seemed to surge.

"I have confidence in you, Balmat. Let's go! For the rest of them, may God have mercy!" Then he began to sing, but not quite in tune. This seemed to worry him.

I took his arm and said, "No one must know of our project except our wives."

However, a third person was obliged to be taken into our confidence. The shopkeeper from whom we bought our supplies was incredulous about what we told her. We invited her to look for us the next morning at about nine o'clock, towards the side of the Dôme du Goûter.

All our little matters being settled, we bid adieu to our wives and departed about five in the afternoon. We set off separately, so no one would know of our plans and met again at a small village. I had brought a coverlet that served to enwrap Paccard as they swathe an infant. Thanks to this precaution, he passed a good night's sleep.

As for me, I slept without waking until one-thirty. At two, the white line appeared and soon the sun arose without a cloud; beautiful and brilliant, promising us a famous journey at last.

In fifteen minutes, we were engaged with the Glacier of Taconnaz. We crossed without incident and soon we left the Grands Mulets below us. I showed the Doctor where I had spent the night. He made a significant grimace and kept silent. We ascended for a bit longer before he suddenly stopped.

"Do you think we will arrive at the top of Mont Blanc today?" he asked.

I saw what he was getting at. He didn't want to spend a night like I had. I reassured him laughingly without promising him anything.

We went on for two hours and reached the Grand Plateau. The wind overtook us and became stronger and stronger with each step. We finally reached the rock of the Petits Mulets. Here, a gust of wind carried away Paccard's hat, even though it was tied on. Hearing his exclamation, I turned around and saw his comfortable cap bounding down towards the town of Courmayeur. He looked as if he were going after it with outstretched arms.

"Bon voyage!" I yelled.

It seemed as if the wind took offense at my joke because a violent blast hit us hard and we were obliged to lie flat on our bellies in order not to follow the hat. We were not able to get up for ten minutes. The wind thrashed the mountain and passed whistling over our heads.

Paccard was discouraged. I thought of the shopkeeper who would be looking to see if we were on the Dôme du Goûter.

At the first respite the wind gave us, I got up. The Doctor would only consent to follow on his hands and knees. In this manner, we pursued the course until we could see the village of Chamonix. At this point, with my glasses, I looked 12,000 feet below us where I made out our "friends" with about fifty others. They were looking up at us through their telescopes. In consideration of his dignity, Paccard got up on his legs. The moment he stood up, we saw that we were recognized by the spectators.

The people in the valley saluted us with their hats. I replied with mine. Paccard had spent all of his energy rising to his feet and did not salute. Encouragement from below or from me failed to induce him into continuing the ascent. After exhausting all my patience and seeing I would only lose time, I told him to keep himself warm and not to stand still. He seemed to listen and numbly replied, "Yes, yes," in order to get rid of me.

I knew he was suffering from the cold. I was almost paralyzed from it. I left him the bottle of water and started off alone, telling him that I would come and fetch him.

"Yes, yes," he replied.

I urged him again not to stand still and off I went. I had not gone thirty paces when I returned and found him, instead of moving about and stamping his feet, sitting down with his back to the glacial wind. I left him with another reminder to move about so that I could continue to ascend.

"Yes, yes."

From this spot, there was no great difficulty to overcome, but the higher I mounted, the less I could breathe. Every ten steps, I was obliged to stop like an asthmatic man. It seemed as if I had no lungs and that my chest was empty. I tied my handkerchief around my mouth and breathed through it and this relieved me a little. The cold had become almost intolerable. It took me an hour to walk a quarter of a league. Still, I went on, with head bent down, until all at once I came to a point I did not recognize. I lifted my head. Lo and behold, I was atop Mont Blanc!

I cast my eyes around, trembling, in case I had deceived myself. My legs seemed to be kept in place only by the aid of my frozen trousers. I was overcome. After so many unfruitful attempts, I had reached the goal of my life where no one had been; not even the eagle or the chamois. I was here without another's aid; only by my will and my strength. All that surrounded me seemed to belong to me.

It was four in the afternoon when I contemplated this giddy panorama. I looked down on Chamonix and I waved my hat. I saw through my glasses that they replied by doing the same.

The first moment of exultation over, I thought of Dr. Paccard. I descended as quickly as possible, calling out his name. I was terrified when he did not answer me. Forty-five minutes had passed. I saw him in the distance, round as a ball, making no movement in spite of my shouts.

I found him with his head between his knees, crouched like a cat. I took him by the shoulder. He raised his head mechanically. I told him that I had reached the summit of Mont Blanc. This news seemed to interest him in the most mediocre way because in reply he asked where he could find a bed and go to sleep. I reminded him that he had come to ascend Mont Blanc and ascend it he should! I raised him up and steered him to walk. The exercise restored his circulation a little and he asked me if I had accidentally put into my pocket the hare-skin gloves that I had made expressly for my ascents. I gave him one of them, though under any other circumstance I would not have given even my brother one!

At six, I was once more on the summit of Mont Blanc with Doctor Paccard. Although the sun still shed bright rays of light, the sky was of a deep dark blue and I could see the stars shining. Below us was ice, snow, rocks, pines; a panorama impossible to describe. I tried to make Paccard a partaker of the spectacle that unfolded itself before our eyes, but it was in vain. He saw nothing. The state he was in deprived him of his morale. The effort to make him enjoy such contemplation was lost.

As for me, I suffered no more; I was no longer fatigued. I scarcely had difficulty breathing when just an hour ago, I had almost abandoned my undertaking. In this state of rapture, I remained on the summit for thirty minutes more.

It was now seven. We had only two more hours of daylight. We had to descend. I took hold of Paccard and I waved my hat as a last signal to the observers in the village. We began our downward journey. There was no track to direct us. The wind was so cold that even the surface of the snow was not melted. All we found here and there on the ice was the small holes that our stocks had made. Paccard was like a child, without energy or will. I guided him in the good parts and carried him over the bad. Night began to fall when we crossed the crevasse at the foot of the Grand Plateau. Each step, Paccard stopped, declaring he could go no further. I made him go on not by persuasion, which he no longer understood, but by sheer force.

At eleven, we left the regions of ice and placed our feet on firm ground. It was more than three hours since we had lost all reflection from the sun. This being the case, I permitted Paccard to rest and when preparing to wrap him again in the coverlet, I found that he did not help me. Upon my remarking this to him, he said, "It is for the best of all reasons. I have no longer any use or feeling in my hands."

I drew off his gloves. His hands were as white as death. As for myself, the hand on which was the leather glove looked like his two. The hand with the hare-skin glove was fine.

I said to him, "Out of four hands, three are of no use." This communication did not interest him. All he desired was to go to sleep.

He managed to say, "Rub the frozen parts with snow."

I began the operation on him and ended it with myself. Soon the circulation was restored as well as warmth, but with it came acute pain, as if each vein were being pricked with needles.

I wrapped "my baby" in his swaddling clothes and we lay down under the shelter of a rock. We ate a morsel and drank a cup of water and lay as close to each other as possible for warmth. There, we fell asleep. The next day at six, I was awakened by Paccard.

"I can hear the birds chirping and singing and yet I cannot see the daylight."

I told him that he was mistaken; that he should be able to see. He then asked for some snow, which he melted in his hands. We mixed it with brandy and applied it to his eyelids. This procedure was to no avail.

"Balmat, I am blind!!"

"It seems very likely, at least right now," I replied.

"How am I to descend?"

"Take hold of the strap of my bag and walk behind me. That is the way!" By this means, we reached the village of Côte.

As I feared that my wife would be anxious, I left the Doctor to find his way home by tapping with his baton and I returned to mine. When my wife saw me, she had such a look of horror that I ran to look at my reflection. I was not recognizable. I had red eyes, a black face and blue lips. Each time I yawned or laughed, blood spurted from my lips.

Four days later, I set out for Geneva to announce the news to de Saussure, but some Englishman had already informed him of my success."

Jacques Balmat did collect the prize and later, on August 3, 1787, he assisted de Saussure himself to reach the summit with a party of about seventeen people.

Balmat was criticized for his account of the climb, particularly since his account downplayed the role of Dr. Paccard. He was considered self-centered, arrogant and exceedingly competitive. Was that because people were jealous of his accomplishment? Either way, all could agree it had taken tremendous

courage – some even say obsession – to make that first
ascent.

Spark

Balmat's account of his ascent intrigued me to learn more about the region. I knew little of the history of the Alpine countries, Swiss liberty or the exiles, saints and martyrs who had once traversed the same paths. I came to recognize this area as the common shrine of Europe.

The early climbs of Mont Blanc were dominated by men, eager to show their courage and determination, but the women of Chamonix were no less interested in climbing. Maria Paradis, a poor maid, harangued Jacques Balmat to assist her in ascending the mountain. They accomplished the summit in 1808. From then on, she was nicknamed "Maria de Mont Blanc" and was rumored to have left out refreshments for others who attempted the climb.

My own wife is captivated by the mountain. She sits for hours staring at its ultimate peak; not in that sad state that has imprisoned her the last few months, but with a keen sense of study and admiration. I can't blame her. The pinnacle and its surrounding peaks rekindle the heart, speak of bright anticipation and reinvigorate the human soul with force and youthful resolution. After several weeks experience, I feel the mountain is trying to claim me. Within myself, I can distinguish successive stages of surrender differing each from the other in character.

Ana constantly reminds me to get outdoors; to not be so chained to the desk. It is a bad and dangerous thing to be deprived of fresh air and exercise, she says. Outside, in Nature's parlor, we inhale the concentrated emanations from the remaining bouquets of flowers and we find ourselves rejuvenated. It feels strange to smile; to hear ourselves laugh; to touch her hand. This mountain air must have drugged us.

As the days become colder, we gather around the fire in our little cabin and discuss our research of the early climbs upon Mont Blanc. We find ourselves strangely spellbound by the region; aware that we are under the spell, but unwilling to fully acknowledge it.

Jacques Balmat had long been a resident of Chamonix. Had his ambition for the monetary reward been the driving force in his ascent or had the mountain been calling to him his entire life? Either way, Balmat had opened the door to a lofty ascent; an invigorating climb, to a place where life is rare and where death is inevitable.

Death

I have thought a lot about death the last several months. Actually, I have been forced to face it. I felt I had arrived at this loss of Sean as a kind of punishment. Was I a good father? Sometimes. Not always. I yelled at Sean when I was irritable. I attempted to control and steer him in a direction he clearly did not want. I didn't always go out with him when he wanted to play ball, surf or bike ride. It seemed like those were things we would do later, down the line, when I had time.

Son, I have all the time in the world for you now. I would give anything to have you back just so you could know that. You died alone, on a cold sidewalk, as your friends scattered, terrified to be blamed for the horrible accident; until a couple of strangers made that call that was just too late to save you. Why did your death have to make me feel your life so deeply? Why did my soul only awaken at your moribund conclusion?

Out here, amongst all this life, there is a thread of death weaved throughout the valley right to the very top of Mont Blanc. A being cannot be enlightened without suffering the pain of loss and this mountain is abundant in its teachings.

Dr. Joseph Hamel's Climb, 1820

One of the great lessons of Mont Blanc was when Dr. Hamel, a Russian physicist, started from Chamonix on August 18, 1820 with two young Englishmen (Messrs. Dornford and Henderson) to make the ascent. Their plan was to test a new oxygen apparatus at the peak. They were detained on August 19th at the Grands Mulets by bad weather. A considerable quantity of snow had fallen on the upper part of the mountain. By eight-twenty, on August 20, 1820 they got to the Grand Plateau. At nine, they continued the march and by ten-thirty, they were somewhere upon the ancient passage above the level of the Dôme du Goûter (14,210 feet) and not much below the top of the Rochers Rouges. Mounting in zigzags to avoid crevasses and to ease the gradients, they pressed on. What happened next was recorded by Mr. Dornford:

> "As we were crossing obliquely a long slope, the snow suddenly gave way beneath our feet. It began at the head of the line and carried us all down the slope to our left. I was thrown instantly off my feet. I then was on my knees and endeavored to regain my footing when, in just a few seconds, the snow on our right rushed into

the gap and suddenly buried us all at once in its mass. The accumulation of snow instantly threw me backwards and I was carried down in spite of my struggles. In less than a minute, I emerged, partly from my own exertion and partly because the velocity of the falling mass had subsided from its own friction. I was obliged to resign my pole in the struggle, feeling it forced out of my hand. A short time afterwards, I found it on the very brink of the crevasse.

At the moment of my emerging, I was so far from being aware of the danger of our situation that upon seeing my two companions up to their waists in snow, and sitting motionless and silent, a joke rose to my lips. But a second glance showed me that, with the exception of Mathieu Balmat (the brother of Pierre Balmat), those two were the only remnants of the party visible. Two more of the party quickly reappeared and I was inclined to treat the affair as a perplexing and ludicrous delay because it had sent us down so many hundred feet lower.

Suddenly, Mathieu Balmat cried out that some of the party were lost and pointed to the crevasse where he said they had fallen. A nearer view convinced us all of the sad truth. The three front guides, Pierre Carrier, Pierre Balmat and Auguste Tairray, being where the slope was somewhat steeper, had all been carried down with great rapidity into the crevasse. Mathieu Balmat, fourth in the line, was a man of great muscular strength as well as presence of mind. He had thrust his pole into the firm snow when he felt himself going over the cliff. This had checked the force of his fall.

One of the back guides who had reappeared, Julien Devouassoux, had been carried into the crevasse where it was very narrow and had been thrown with some violence against the opposite brink. He scrambled out without assistance and sustained a small cut on the chin. The other guide, JM Coutet, had been dragged out by his companions. He was quite senseless and nearly black with frostbite from the weight of snow that had been upon him. In a short time, however, he recovered.

It was a long time before we could convince ourselves that the others were past hope and we exhausted ourselves, for some time, in fathoming the loose snow with our poles. The first few minutes we spent in a frantic attempt to recover them. After being thoroughly convinced that the poor fellows were indeed in the crevasse as pointed out by Mathieu Balmat, who was after all the brother of Pierre, only one thing remained to be done and that was to venture down and return to the Grands Mulets. Fortunately, it did not give way beneath our weight. Here, we continued to make every exertion in our power for the recovery of our poor comrades. After thrusting our poles in to their full length, we knelt down and shouted along them, listening for an answer. But all was as silent as the grave."

It is not evident from the narratives of this affair where the avalanche started. Dornford later mentioned being hurried "downwards toward two crevasses about a furlong below." JM Coutet, in one of his accounts, said that he was carried two hundred meters below some of the others and in another place he speaks of going down four hundred feet in a minute and then of flying through the air.

The probability seems to be that the five guides who were in front were carried a considerable distance down the slope and then shot over the ice cliffs. The three leading men were lost and completely buried up in the crevasse by the snow they had dislodged. JM Coutet and Julien Devouassoux very narrowly escaped the same fate.

Ten years later, when conducting a climbing party by the corridor route, Coutet pointed in the direction of the crevasse that had nearly swallowed him whole. He somberly stated, "They are there."

All the guides seemed to deeply feel the loss of their ill-fated comrades and thought that in all probability they would remain embedded beneath the Grand Plateau. But by that time (1830), the bodies were no doubt already a considerable distance from the spot where the accident occurred, because the dismembered remains of the three unfortunates re-appeared at the lower end of the Glacier des Bossons in 1861, more than four miles away, in a direct line, from the place where they perished. They must have travelled downwards on an average rate of five hundred feet per annum.

"I never would have thought that," said JM Coutet, who was still living when these vestiges of the catastrophe were discovered.

Fragments of skulls (one of which was identified as that of Pierre Balmat), a lower part of an arm with its hand, fragments of knapsacks, a felt hat (worn by Carrier), a crampon, a tin lantern, shreds of clothing and a cooked leg of mutton were among the objects that came to light first.

Later, in 1862, a multitude of other articles were found; part of the remains is interred at Chamonix as reminders of the lives claimed by Mont Blanc.

Desire

The horrible deaths of the three gifted guides did not dissuade the lovers of the climb. The mountain demands more life upon it and climbers were still determined to ascend the peak. More significantly, I began to discover, from studying historical accounts, that the mountain deeply affected those who attained the peak. Yet, even in the lower regions, I was undergoing profound changes and I needed to learn more about the experiences of others. Five separate written accounts exist from men who detail their strange desires, altered mental state or spiritual experiences upon the mountain. I began by studying the account of Sherwill and Clark.

Ascent of Sherwill & Clark, as told by
Dr. Clark, 1824 and 1825

"On a beautiful serene summer evening, a group of us walked up the hill from the town of Neuchatel to La Rochelte, a charming villa overhanging the lake. Standing there on the terrace walk, you look down over a green vineyard, a poplar colonnade and the blue surface of the lake. Beyond rises the green swelling hills of the opposite shore and then, far above, the eye roams along a snowy range of Swiss and Savoy Alps extending more than a hundred miles in the sweep of the distant horizon. Surrounded with exotics of the gayest tint and sweetest fragrance, we gazed for the first time on the hoary monarch of the Alps, Mont Blanc.

The sun gradually descended behind the mountain range. We watched in silence the shadow of the horizon spreading slowly upwards from peak to peak. When all the less lofty summits were clad in sober grey, the colossal summit of Mont Blanc remained conspicuous, like a bright cloud detached from the earth. It was glowing with a warm roseate light in the last rays of sunset.

The first view of this splendid panorama is certainly one of the strongest, most expansive and most delicious sensations of life. Few scenes have a deep impressive hold on the memory as Mont Blanc. If we were looking for a simile to convey some faint notion of this peculiar glow of the mountain at sunset, we might feebly express it as phosphorus glowing with mitigated light on a cloudy day.

Approaching Geneva near Malagny, we again enjoyed this gorgeous spectacle. Often, by the lake of Geneva and its lovely environs, we saw Mont Blanc at sunset, but never do I recall having seen it tinged with so deep a ruby glow as on that evening. To observe it more attentively, we ran up through a vineyard and gazed in silent admiration as it evolved from a bright ruby red into a deep violet.

Determined to ascend the mountain, I returned at the end of August, 1824 and took up quarters at the excellent Hotel de l'Union at Chamonix, close to the base of the mountain. The weather, however, proved unpropitious. Having waited several days during which all the high summits were covered with incessant mist, I decided to leave. Upon departure, I saw the immense colossal form of the white giant lifting his hoary head in awful majesty, claiming his rightful reverence as indisputable sovereign of the European hills. I lingered there, feasting my eyes next on the sublime spectacle of the huge Dôme du Goûter. The vast slopes of snow glittered like silver in the glorious burst of sunshine.

While crossing the noble river Po, I said a long farewell to the Alps, intending to return a year later to make the climb.

Back in Geneva, I had a conversation with a friend about the disastrous attempt of Dr. Hamel in 1820. It was deeply impressed upon me that to hazard the climb without the advice of the experienced guides would not only be childish, but a base and selfish trifling with human life. My first visit was therefore directed to the bureau of the Chief Guide, Monsieur Simon.

Further, my friend strongly warned me against attempting so long a journey without much previous exercise. He was accustomed to alpine marches on his botanizing excursions and spoke from experience. No man can walk from thirty to forty miles on ice and snow until he is slowly habituated to the exertion. The numerous and unsuccessful efforts to ascend Mont Blanc have probably failed by inattention to this circumstance than by any other cause.

When I returned to Chamonix in August, 1825, I immediately went to see Monsieur Simon, having previously written to him, warning him of my arrival and asking for his help. Upon meeting the kind-faced man, I begged him to give me his unqualified judgment as to the practicability of the ascent, promising to acquiesce in his decision whatever that might be. He smiled sweetly and moved slowly, his nimble fingers toying with an old clock as he digested my request.

Finally, Simon replied, "When the weather is favorable, I like nothing better than to form one of the party. When I was a young man, I made the attempt, but we did not succeed. Since having married, I have not renewed the experiment, simply from unwillingness to disoblige my family."

That objection did not apply to me, so I asked Simon how soon it might be proper to ascend. His answer was less satisfactory. He said that at present the matter was impracticable.

They had some recent snowfall on the upper parts of the mountain which would require several days of continued sunshine to harden it. Simon said he would let me know as soon as the weather appeared sufficiently settled. In the meantime, he recommended several preparatory mountain excursions both to ascertain the physical strength of my chosen party and to augment the stock.

In obedience to the advice of Simon, I set out early on a beautiful summer morning to begin our training exercises with the gifted guide, Julien Devouassoux. He was such an amiable character, full of jokes and laughter, but deadly serious whenever we encountered trouble. He was swarthy; his accent so thick that I struggled to understand him, but he always made the effort to make sure I did.

Of course, the training exercise was for my benefit, not the already well-conditioned Julien. We ascended the Montanvert, descended to the Mer de Glace, traversed its whole length and dined on the celebrated Jardin. It is a small pyramidal islet of grass and flowers enclosed on all sides by a sea of ice and snow, but the point of view is sublime beyond words. Julien told me about his wife and children, of whom he was very proud.

In traversing the plains of ice, we found great advantage from the use of double-headed ice-screws fixed into the heel of the shoe. These gave us great security and firmness, both in walking and leaping the chasms and no traveler should neglect this simple precaution.

So invigorating is the high mountain air, coupled with the strong stimulus of sublime and perfectly novel scenery, that on returning, we were little fatigued. In the evening, by starlight, I walked with Julien about five miles to examine a barometer possessed by JM Coutet. We spent some time examining it and going over the little manipulations. It had never mounted to the summit, so it was resolved that should the weather continue to steady enough to admit our ascent, Coutet should go with us. The finding of such an excellent instrument at Chamonix was gratifying and Coutet consented to go.

We were lucky to have JM Coutet agree to the expedition. With legs like giant blocks of granite, Coutet was the most experienced guide; a man with eyes sharper than an eagle and a mind quicker than a hummingbird. His ability was remarkable, having ascended the mountain more than any other man alive.

At about ten that night, Julien returned with me to the inn. There was no moon and a sudden mountain torrent had torn up the road and covered the plain with sand and granite blocks. Unfortunately, this had done great damage to Julien's home so he, his wife and children had to find shelter at the inn. Despite this, the day had been exceedingly delightful and we began to feel sanguine of success and anxiously desired to make the expedition.

The following morning, however, the scene had altered. The glittering chain of gigantic peaks had disappeared; all was one thick mass of clouds and dense fog. Around noon, the sun again appeared and we seized the opportunity to ascend La Flegere, a mountain opposite the Mer de Glace. Superb as this view is, to us it was less interesting than the previous day's ramble to Jardin.

We had then a beautifully clear morning and with a telescope, we could very distinctly see and examine the state of the ice and snows on Mont Blanc. The guides concluded, after a careful and anxious survey, that the glacier beneath the Grands Mulets was unusually cracked and fissured.

In the evening, the weather once more changed. Some snow fell on the higher mountains and the Chief Guide gave us very little hope of trying the ascent during this season.

Nothing is more uncertain than the climate of Chamonix. When we had lost all hope, the sky all of a sudden resumed its clearness. On one of the most heavenly mornings possible, without a single streak or cloud, a few of us set off on mules to ascend the Buet, the highest mountain in this part of the chain as part of a training exercise.

I had the great pleasure of being accompanied by a young doctor (the son of a distinguished physician in London) whom I had met in the village. He had recently passed over land from India and we talked of the torrid sands of Arabia while plodding our way along the eternal snows of the Alps. One would never know he had encountered some of the hottest places on Earth because his skin was clear, smooth and pale as that of a baby. His wavy flax-blonde hair framed his stunning watery green eyes.

The clearness of the sky, the amazing extent and wildness of the prospect, our amusing glissades down slopes of snow, the feeling of augmenting muscular strength, and above all, the companionship, made it the most pleasant ramble I had ever enjoyed.

When I got back to the village, Julien thought it prudent to set out immediately on the expedition to Mont Blanc, but on calm consultation with Simon, we determined we should not set out until the weather was more fixed. I went back to tell my new friend, but found he was determined to leave Chamonix.

During our blissful time on the Buet, emotions and actions had overcome me and my doctor friend when we found ourselves alone together. He now was ashamed, angry and confused. These events compelled him to suddenly leave the village and I gave up all hope of finding another companion for the expedition.

I went back to see Monsieur Simon and meet with the five guides selected to head out the morning of the 24th of August. JM Coutet and Julien consented to go then, but the prudent Monsieur Simon strongly urged waiting one more day. The new snows might be more firmly agglutinated to the old by then. Although afraid the weather might change again, we delayed for one more day; albeit in more than a little frustration. This pause gave me time to think about my friend and what desires had overcome us on our ramble together. I felt heartbroken over his departure.

That same day, our arrangements nearly complete for starting out the following morning, the brash Captain Markham Sherwill arrived in Chamonix. Upon finding JM Coutet, he hired him and they ascended to the Mer de Glace. Coutet must have told him of my plans because immediately upon returning to the inn, Captain Sherwill proposed to me to join my expedition. I thought it fair to mention to him the necessity of preparatory mountain courses and strength training before such an endeavor, but Captain Sherwill conceived this training was unnecessary for him.

With his dark curly hair and a mustache to match, Sherwill seemed a bit reckless, with a mischievous twinkle in his eye. He was also a keen womanizer, distracted by several females in the village; but, he sounded sincere in his resolve to summit Mont Blanc. He was also most keen on obtaining autographs from all the guides and many of the other climbers in the village.

We decided to hire two additional guides and agreed that if either of us wanted to return, it would then be considered fair and honorable that the other should take four of the seven guides and proceed onwards.

We set out to procure the two additional guides. This, however, was difficult. Of the forty guides enrolled at Chamonix, only half could be induced to think of the ascent; and of those who were disposed to go, the greater part were already hired. There was an unusual amount of travelers at that time in the valley. The deliberation and adjustment of the list of guides was the most painful part of the whole preparation. It was impossible not to feel that, in writing down the name of a guide on a scrap of paper, you might unintentionally be doing him an injury.

At last, however, the affair was finally arranged. I had already frequently debated with the guides on the best mode of dividing the journey. At first, I had proposed to sleep on the Rochers Rouges the first night so we might have an abundance of time to spare upon the summit. This motion, however, was unanimously rejected and the opinion quite decisive that the nights were now too long and too cold to think of sleeping at so high an elevation. Even Coutet declared that nothing could tempt him to renew so hazardous an experiment.

The next proposition was to encamp for the night on the Grand Plateau, leaving the ascent of the steep slope towards the Rochers Rouges until the morning. To this plan Coutet was less averse, but Julien strongly opposed the motion, even declaring that if we were to advance beyond the Grands Mulets, he must be excused from joining the party. I did not have the least doubt that Julien spoke from a strong conviction because he had proved himself an intrepid and very attentive guide, but I was disconcerted by his refusal. I was now convinced that no traveler should think of sleeping on the Grand Plateau the first night. To do so is to tempt fate. Even with the finest possible weather and the utmost exertion, it would be no easy task to reach the summit and return before night. A shower of rain or the most trifling accident would have proved rather serious.

After much discussion, we consented to encamp the first night on the Grands Mulets. Coutet reminded us that we might need to terminate our excursion, which he said had happened to him on many occasions before.

Dr. Michel Paccard, who first ascended Mont Blanc with J. Balmat, and still resided at Chamonix, was good enough to show me the crampons he used in that expedition, but I thought the ice-screws far simpler and better.

A caretaker at the inn, Mrs. Simond, a plump woman with a maternal kindness that I shall not easily forget, first scolded us for even thinking of the excursion and then set to work to provide every little comfort she could possibly procure or manufacture. A pencil was jammed into the bun of her gray hair which she removed frequently to cross another item off her list.

On Thursday, August 25, 1825, I awakened at five with news of a delightful morning. I dressed as usual, putting on a pair of shoes with large pyramidal nails and a pair of strong gaiters made for the occasion, lined with Chamois leather. Descending to the room below, we found our party of guides leisurely having breakfast, however, there reigned a share of gravity on all faces. No one seemed in a hurry. How could they be? Today might be their last day on Earth.

The provisions were already packed and sent on by porters to the edge of the glacier, where we were to breakfast. About five minutes after seven we mounted our two mules and bid farewell to our friends and a numerous circle of the old guides who had assembled to see us set out. Among them was the fine and vigorous old man, Jacques Balmat, the first man to ascend Mont Blanc.

Our excellent landlord bid us goodbye with the most cordial wishes for our success; and the kind-hearted Madame Simond shook us by the hand with tears in her eyes, repeating frequently that she had not given her consent to our expedition.

Captain Sherwill and I left the hotel accompanied by the following seven guides on foot:

1. JM Coutet, married, aged 35; had been up six times; was nearly killed by the avalanche in Dr. Hamel's attempt.

2. Simeon Devouassoux, aged 30, married, 1 child. Once to the summit.

3. Jean-Pierre Tairraz; aged 38, single. Once to the summit.

4. Julien Devouassoux, aged 36, married, 3 children. Never to the summit; nearly killed by the avalanche in 1820.

5. Pierre-Joseph Simond, aged 37, married, 1 child. Never to the summit.

6. Simon Tournier, aged 28, single. Never to the summit.

7. Michel Devouassoux, aged 26, married, 2 children. Never to the summit.

We immediately crossed over the bridge of the Arve, and then along the left bank of the river by the mule road, through fields of hemp, corn, flax, etc. We passed over the waste of sand

and granite blocks caused by the torrent that had utterly devastated Julien's little farm.

At seven-thirty, we arrived at Coutet's chalet and dismounted to examine the barometers and compare the scales. David Coutet, brother of JM Coutet, was hired to examine the instruments at appointed times while we were above. Coutet put on his hussar jacket and wide coarse straw hat, bid a hasty adieu to his weeping wife and we left.

As we began to ascend, Julien walked close to my mule and said half-serious, half-smiling, "I assure you, we have prepared well."

We crossed a little rivulet then entered a pleasant wood of firs, and soon, emerging from the pine wood, commenced a steep winding passage among the mountain shrubs. On our right, we had the edge of the long white Glacier des Bossons and on our left, the stream from the Cascade des Pelerins. This path gradually led up to the last patch of cultivation surrounding another guide's cottage.

It was now eight-thirty with a beautiful blue sky. Sitting on the mule, we halted a few minutes to rest the guides. Looking directly down, you saw under your feet the dark pine woods at the base of the mountain intersected by the white stony torrent that had burst itself into several channels to join the Arve. Further on, numerous brown chalets dispersed irregularly among the parallel stalks of yellow corn, green hemp, flax and clover. Further up, the huge bulk of the Dôme du Goûter shined like polished silver in the morning sun. Very anxiously we examined the white masses of clouds in the distant horizon.

We alighted from our mules, and entered the last human habitation we were to pass, the chalet of a man named Favret. The good old man was not at home; but a pleasing young woman, I believe his daughter, gave us some excellent goat's milk. There were two females there busy in their domestic cares while a wood fire warmed the place. Captain Sherwill and the other guides were ogling their plump breasts and ample rear ends. I walked over to the fire to examine a monstrous black kettle that was suspended on a cumbrous wooden crane used for boiling milk, making cheese, etc. The roof sloped rapidly down, supported on low walls of uncemented stone and a projection of the same roof covered a goat's shed, which was only slightly separated from the living quarters. In a corner were two makeshift beds.

Having finished our milk, we bid adieu to our young hostess, who wished us success with a good-natured smile.

On we went as the mules scrambled nimbly from rock to rock. Julien showed us a spot where he had nearly perished from mistakenly drinking a small quantity of sulphuric acid during Dr. Hamel's expedition of 1820.

About nine forty-five, we left the mules at a dwelling called La Pierre Pointue. It is a kind of stone tent formed of a vast block on one side and a wall of uncemented stone on the side next the glacier. The mouth is open, but once inside you are tolerably snug. Here, the solitary goat herder and part of his flock find occasional shelter from the pelting storm and biting blasts of wind.

The road being no longer at all practicable for mules, we sent them back with pencil notes to our friends below, written by a fine ruddy-cheeked smiling child of the mountain.

Advancing rapidly on foot, we passed by a narrow goat track among rhododendron shrubs overhanging a steep acclivity of several hundred feet. There was, however, no considerable danger, as long as you were cautious in placing your feet.

At ten forty-five, we reached the extreme edge of vegetation and were on the verge of the broad moraine of stones that skirt the glacier. Here, we were not sorry to find the porters had already arrived with the baggage and breakfast. The important materials were hastily unpacked; two napkins spread out for us upon a rock; some water brought up from a stream of melted ice, and a few wine bottles were uncorked.

We sat down to breakfast under the influence of the keen mountain air. As we sat, munching very diligently, loud rumbling shocks were heard from time to time and every now and then, a long distant roar of an avalanche.

The summit of the Brevent appeared to be about level with us and upon its top we could distinctly see several travelers who had ascended to watch our progress. With our telescope we made out their signal to us: a hat placed on a baton, which we hastened to answer by a counter-signal.

The round snowy top of the Buet now reared itself above the line of the Aiguilles Rouges. Beneath, in the distance, we watched the deep bed of the Arve River until it wound around and plunged from sight into a dark fir-covered ravine. A little higher up, we distinctly made out part of the stream that runs down to form the lovely Cascade de Chede.

When we had some time to rest, I was desirous of examining the rate of the pulse of the party; and found the pulse of one of the oldest porters, named Coutet le Chamois (no relation to our guide Coutet) beat at eighty-four; our lead guide Coutet, eighty-four; my own, eighty-eight; the guide, Simeon Devouassoux, ninety-two; and Captain Sherwill, one hundred and eight. This result surprised me a good deal. I had expected to find the pulse of the strongest and most muscular subjects least accelerated. This, however, did not appear to be the case as Jean-Pierre Tairraz, a young Hercules in figure and muscle, had a pulse fourteen beats quicker than my own.

When we finished our breakfast, Julien amused himself by firing a pistol so that we might hear the echo. It was not remarkable and probably the concussion helped to accelerate an avalanche, which fell some time after at this spot.

The sky still looked a little hazy in the horizon, but the guides seemed sanguine. The opinion was general that the desired north wind would continue. Our eye was now fixed on the dark rocks of Mont Maudit. It was embedded in snowy steeps and beneath them resembled a small narrow islet in the wide expanse of ice and snow.

Now, all was bustle and business. All being ready, the porters bid us goodbye and prepared to descend. One of them, however, begged hard to join the upland party and the guides were desirous that he should go, in order to lessen the proportion of baggage to each. This was the old porter Coutet le Chamois. He said he had been a crystal hunter and that he had acquired his name from his dexterity and courage in precipitous passages. He further claimed he had once been alone to the summit of Mont Blanc and had come down to Chamonix at eight in the evening, having left the top at noon. He also said that the snows were then very good and that he slid down the frozen slopes with his baton, going swift as lightning.

This report of his solitary ramble was received with a sly shrug by the other guides and evidently held to be a little apocryphal. However, at the old man's strong request, it was determined that he should join our party and receive proportionate compensation.

As we now had only a small space before leaving terra firma and entering on the ice, I took off the shoes used in ascending the mountain and put on a thicker pair made for the occasion, well furnished with double-headed ice screws. These I had kept in reserve, fearing to wear down, on the hard granite, the points of the screws. In leaping a chasm, or passing on its edge, a bent or faulty screw might easily induce a final slip.

In a few minutes, we had crossed the moraine of granite blocks and (perhaps with a little more anxiety than we cared to display) abandoned solid Mother Earth. We then embarked on the troubled ocean of ice.

Having scarcely advanced two hundred yards, we found ourselves involved in a labyrinth of icy walls from fifteen to thirty feet high and separated by chasms of unknown depth. The ice-axe was in active operation as the lead guide had to test the solidity of the tottering bridges or cut footsteps where the walls were too steep to be ascended. In scaling these slippery barriers, we mounted from hole to hole and from crag to crag, sometimes climbing on hands and knees, at other times gratefully receiving the end of a staff or the handle of the ice-axe to assist in mounting to a ledge of ice, overhanging a chasm of not a very inviting aspect.

This kind of scrambling march was much more laborious and more dangerous than anything we had done on our other mountain rambles and I felt a queer delight in acting like a madman. The guides' jovial demeanor further prevented my feelings of serious apprehension.

We were all quite silent, only attending to the immediate business at hand. It soon became very evident that our new party member, the old porter, had grossly overrated his remaining strength. Far from being able to assist us, it was found necessary to assist him. The spirited old mountaineer insisted that he was perfectly able to bear the fatigue, but we all persuaded him to renounce the enterprise.

Julien kindly accompanied him a little way back to give him a hand in descending a steep crag. We lost sight of the old man's slouched hat as he gaily leapt off an icy wall to regain the rocks.

I wondered what had possessed him to think he could make this climb at his advanced age. Yet, there was much to admire about the delicacy the younger guides had begged the old man to return. There was no rude jesting or unfeeling laughter; only kind and soothing expressions. This considerate and amiable geniality was particularly remarkable in one of the guides, Simeon Devouassoux. His treatment of the old porter alone convinced me that he would turn out a brave man. He was kind and thoughtful, but well aware of the dangers of our ascent. Feeling implicit confidence in his direction, I selected him as my personal guide and his unwearied attention, his calm courage, soothing demeanor and persevering exertion contributed materially to the pleasure and the safety of our excursion.

With the old porter now having safely returned to the valley below, his share of the baggage was distributed among the original seven guides. The party again set forward, steering as directly as possible towards the Grands Mulets. Very rarely, however, could we advance in a straight line, the course being incessantly traversed by crevices and chasms from a few inches to twenty-five or thirty feet in width and generally of fearful depth. We were therefore obliged to wind backwards and forwards to seek the safest passages. Coutet, Simeon, Julien and Tairraz (a man of great enthusiasm) were constantly ahead, sometimes widely separated from one another.

We had not yet put on our ropes so that the leading guides were occasionally in situations where one slip would have been certain death. It was not very comfortable to see the foremost man, with an axe in his hand and a heavy sack on his back, silently stepping along the ridge of a narrow wall of ice with a blue chasm some two hundred or three hundred feet deep, gaping on each side of him. It was, moreover, unsettling to surrender complete trust in the guides to cut a safe passage. I had to constantly remind myself these were experienced mountaineers.

Cautiously and slowly we advanced, often only ten yards; so completely were we hemmed in at times by perpendicular walls of ice. At one place, we found ourselves deep down in a sort of icy crack, with so steep a wall before us that for some time the exit was wholly a mystery. At last, we were extremely happy in discovering a beautiful natural vault through which we all crept and then scrambled up on the top of the ice that formed this curious arch.

The state of the glacier was unusually bad this summer. The guides universally declared they had never seen it more fissured and cleft. Coutet said that in some seasons, we should have passed over this part of our journey in half the time and with a quarter the difficulty.

For some time, our progress was so slow and there was now and then a little whispering among the guides that made us fear the difficulties were insurmountable and we would be compelled to return. The chasms appeared at first view absolutely impassable and were only at last overcome by great personal hazard and labor on the part of the guides. Our step became firmer and nimbler and the cracks narrower, and less numerous, so that we got on much faster and the ticklish passages became rather a matter of amusement than of anxiety as now and again our laughter rang out.

Our attention was incessantly excited by the wild whimsical outline of the icy crags. In a little deep pool, surrounded on all sides by high walls of ice, we found some water. The guides rightly conjectured that this would be the last water we would find unfrozen, and, being very thirsty, we halted to take a copious draught.

As we stood in a group at the bottom of this little dell, the view on every side was exceedingly odd and beautiful. In one direction, the outline of the icy circle was wildly rent down and cleft; in another, curiously jagged and contorted; in another, rising into lofty pinnacles or jutting out into promontories of a pale azure green, dripping fast under the powerful rays of the afternoon sun.

I attempted to take a few hasty sketches in my notebook as the guides were finishing their libations, but neither words nor pencil can convey a clear conception of the wildness and singularity of the forms.

We were now approaching the junction of the Glacier de Taconnaz with the Glacier des Bossons. The disorder and confusion in the masses were evidently produced by the lateral pressure of these huge frozen seas on each other.

As we were plodding quietly along the snow, absorbed in silent wonder, our footsteps were suddenly arrested by a loud roar, like that of distant heavy artillery. Every eye turned towards the sound and with shuddering emotion, we saw the dust of a vast avalanche of tons of ice and snow falling to the base of the Aiguille du Midi to the area where we had halted for breakfast. Coutet and the guides appeared shaken as this naturally brought to mind the fatal disaster of 1820. The question arose to my mind, "What am I doing here?"

It was comforting to see we were on an open slope of broken ice covered with a pretty thick stratum of snow. We had "nothing" to fear but concealed chasms. We marched on rapidly; and, about three, we saw with great pleasure, over the summit of the Brevent, the quiet lake of Geneva shining like a vast mirror in the low hazy distance. In about an hour, we began to draw nearer to the Grands Mulets. The snow was now deeper, occasionally to the knee. We crossed three or four natural bridges of ice lightly spanning a dark gulf. The guides warned us to tread carefully in their footsteps and every one passed as gently and as quickly as possible, holding his ice-pole under his arm. The crevices around the base of the Grands Mulets have always been represented as the most formidable in the whole passage and as the cracks on entering the glacier were unusually deep and numerous, it was anticipated that we might find it impossible to mount on the rocks at all and be compelled to encamp on the snows. Simeon said this had happened to him on a previous journey.

We were anxious to examine these chasms. On first view, their appearance was not very prepossessing. We were encouraged by Coutet's remark that, upon the whole, they were less formidable than he had feared. We advanced slowly along the slippery margin; but, after several awkward passages, suddenly came to a complete standstill upon a sort of corner of ice projecting into a chasm of fearful depth and width. This seemed at first to be a barrier to further progress. A council was called and we stood in anxious debate nearly up to our knees in snow on the edge of the gulf.

Coutet said that when the crevices proved bad, he preferred making a considerable circuit so as to avoid the principal chasms and also escape a very steep and difficult passage of rock at the base of the Grands Mulets. He proposed to dispatch a party to see whether we could pass the crack by steering a little more to the right, towards the base of the Dôme du Goûter. Simeon and Julien immediately set out on the errand for we had no time to lose.

They were soon hidden from sight, having descended some distance into another branch of the chasm. They were concealed from us for some time and we began to feel uneasy.

We were glad when they reappeared, though with somewhat long faces. They reported that the crack widened so it would be absolute madness to think of crossing it in that direction. Coutet still seemed rather of the opinion that it might be as well to return on our steps and make yet a wider circuit to avoid passing the crevice. His opinion was not generally popular.

Our feet were now getting so bitterly cold from standing still in the snow, that the prospect of reaching solid rock and thereby getting our feet off the ice was exceedingly alluring. From the spot where we stood, the steep passage at the base of the Grands Mulets did not appear very difficult, but we afterwards found it far more so than we had reckoned.

The prevailing opinion was to make at once for the rocks, which were but a few hundred yards from the corner of ice on which we stood in consultation. After diligent search, a sort of narrow bridge of ice was found that facilitated the passage considerably, although it was still nerve-wracking.

The lead guide, attached to a cord, cut holes as he passed. When he had secured himself, another guide cautiously followed to the same slippery landing place. In like manner, we had to make our way and with a little sliding, crawling, and jumping, we were all on the other side of the principal crack. This maneuver we repeated two or three times, but it was not altogether comfortable. Anxiety was on every face and conversation was monosyllabic.

After about twenty minutes of scrambling, we stepped with great satisfaction from the surface of the glacier to a projecting mass of rock. The first sensation of placing the foot upon the solid and comparatively warm surface of the rock was quite luxurious and the muscles were relieved from that incessant tension necessary in walking upon ice.

Having all reached the base of the Grands Mulets, the next affair was to ascend them and this was a work of time and fatigue. Coutet and Simeon estimated the height of the steep part at about 250 feet. It did not appear to me by any means that much, but it was certainly the most rapid ascent I ever crawled up; perpendicular, of course. The masses of rock were sometimes loose and it was necessary to examine with great care the stability of a block before trusting your weight onto it. The guide in advance endeavored to direct us where to place our hands or feet; and, in very ticklish parts, he let down the end of his rope, which you tied around your chest then crept forward, and were now and then dragged upwards by sheer muscular effort.

Our progress up was slow. It was about half an hour when we found ourselves all safe and sound on the upper part of the Grands Mulets. Long faces were now shortened and anxious silence exchanged for gaiety and jokes. Julien,

Coutet (also a natural jokester) was in high glee and Michel, the youngest of the guides with a set of dark blue eyes I won't soon forget, joined in the joke sparring.

The first business was to scrape out most of the snow with a flat stone and then to turn up the dry sides of the other flat stones which served as a mattress. A single blanket was then spread and having put on dry shoes, gaiters, etc., we sat down very snugly. The guides now fell to work to light up a fire of some pieces of wood, which were found at the edge of the glacier and had been brought up for the purpose. An old ladder was found on the rocks, left here exposed since last year, and no longer serviceable. Julien cut up part of it into shavings as dexterously as an old seaman would have done and we soon had a wreathing column of smoke and a cheerful blaze that enlivened the whole scenery.

No water was found anywhere on the rocks; the great black copper saucepan was therefore piled up with snow and melted. Some wine and sugar greatly improved the potion. The knapsacks were hastily unpacked and we began supper with much appetite and peals of laughter at the oddness of our situation and personal appearance.

After supper, the guides concocted a mixture of snow, brandy, lemons and sugar as we watched the evening approach. Suddenly, we were all roused to our feet by the loud roar of an avalanche falling very near us. A prodigious mass of soft, loose snow slipped from the impending heights of Mont Maudit into the deep narrow valley at the foot of the Grands Mulets. Standing on our sleeping shelf, we could watch the rapid motion of the mass. It continued falling several seconds and a large cloud of snowy dust rushed nearly halfway across the valley.

We were highly delighted at seeing a large avalanche and not being in its path. It was one of the grandest I had ever seen, large and sublime, like rapids of liquid silver. The deep valley filled with those immense cubes of snow in a wild and chaotic scene.

As night advanced, the scene became increasingly beautiful. We saw Lake Geneva looking increasingly bright as the surrounding hills grew grey in the shades of evening.

Far, far above us, the snowy summit of Mont Blanc still receded in distant majesty but upon looking at it, we felt we had not come much closer to the top. There was hardly a breath of wind; all was hushed and still as death. We gazed until the scene grew dim in twilight and then sat down on our stony couch. A second blanket was spread as a covering; three poles were placed in an inclined position against the rock, and to them was attached a sheet to form a rude tent over our heads. The song of the guides had ceased; their evening prayers were said and we all went to sleep, as best we could. Every now and then the low distant roar of an avalanche roused our attention. The stones that formed our couch were uneven and angular and the air was very chill, though less so than we had expected.

Captain Sherwill slept little, distressed by nausea, but I was able to fall asleep. I soon felt myself being dragged out of the tent by my ankles. I went limp, allowing it to happen rather than question what force was pulling me across the stony shelf. I knew I was merely dreaming, but there was something delicious in feeling as if I was awake. I opened one eye, for fun, and nearly choked on my horror. I was on the edge of a stony cliff!

I scrambled back to a level area and sat crouched like a panther, searching for my abductor. But I was alone; all was silent except for the snores of the climbing party. I had nearly tipped over a cliff to my death and I could not account for why or how I had ended up there. My ankles were sore from the grip that had been placed upon them.

The dark sky was perfectly clear with the stars sparkling in the ebony vault. To complete the sublimity of the scene, the bright moon was shining on the top of Mont Blanc and throwing strong masses of light and shade over the wide waste of snow. This image alone was worth the pilgrimage.

I was overcome by the solemn and awful wildness of the moonlit scene. I thought of those who had died on this climb. There was a certain attraction and reverence to being named one of its victims; like a decorated fallen soldier.

This mountain summoned me and I came willingly, eagerly; even a bit crazily. Something had brought me to this ledge and I had allowed it. I had yet to ascend the ultimate peak, but I knew I would.

When long chained-down to the pursuit of status and wealth, the human spirit shrinks from the vast contemplation of life and mortality. But out here, amidst the awful monuments of a power unseen, the dreams of material objects seduce no more. They are just no longer relevant. Here, man feels himself as a worm, an insect, an atom; he is but a speck in the grand creation. Strangely, with this knowledge of my insignificance, dangling on a ledge facing death, I no longer am afraid to *live*."

Life

As Dr. Clark had written, Ana and I also experienced feeling less afraid in the grand scheme that is life; even though our climbs have been limited to the lower mountain peaks. Ana has never been a hard or angry woman, but the grief over our son had definitely blackened her mood. Early on, when we first arrived, she wrote in her journal of her darker experience with the mountain:

"On the mountainside, as we climbed under a sky black with accumulated snows, the most radiant horizons veiled themselves in gloom. We could see the sinister shadows fall on a field of ruins below and hear the keen north wind hissing. Yet, this was tempting. To confront the wind, to strive against obstacles, to push on despite great fatigue, my heart beat with a strange savage joy. Having nothing but myself and Nature colliding soul to soul was to feel as if I had acquired wings and was an ecstasy pure and delightful as it was brief. And in the midst, the question arose: Can I easily ascend from this point? My leaping heart contracted and the power of respiration seemed to fail me in that moment. The green glacier gazed at me with its fixed dull eye, taunting me. The falling stones threatened to crush me while at intervals sounded the most frightful detonations. They proceeded from abysses opening in its sides. If I dared to explore them, they would surely engulf me. What I supposed to be peace was but a treacherous immobility. What I thought to be an increase of life would speedily prove my death. The air, which at a lower level nourishes me, was here too rarefied and I found it difficult to breathe. I hoped to see the sky open, but I saw only darkness. I was overwhelmed. Nature had not erected her temple up there. She, who seems everywhere else to be our mother, up here seems to be our enemy. The scene is too powerful for the gaze; its mystery is too terrible and its labor is too overwhelming. There is a reason it is coined the hermit. This peak wants to be left alone."

Her perspective is now changing. Mont Blanc, even its lower regions, demands respect and we began to feel the seriousness of it without our hearts being heavy because the keen sense of life is too raw to make us feel depressed. Ana is changing rapidly and I am eager to follow her into the light. I relish the brightness I see in her blue eyes.

For most of my life, flowers, clouds, trees and the like have had no effect upon me and I have been the poorer for it. I am learning all of these softer sentiments from Ana here in Chamonix as she surrenders to its natural charm. This is her great power, which she wisely exercises. She has become the perfect physician; creating day by day health and harmonious equilibrium and barring the door against dark gloomy thoughts.

We take advantage of these beautiful hours; these precious excursions. We walk under majestic pines that enclose us with their furry embrace. In her black hair she weaves the blue blossoms she had pressed and preserved before winter descended upon us. Ana encourages me to listen to the whispers spoken in the rustling trees. Nature, every day, enriches her with strength, embellishes her with a luxury of life, and makes a magic charm of her.

A woman of a pure and lofty heart and of an enlightened will, Ana seems by that very purity to be a worthy offering to the imperious mountain. Have I gone mad that I wish to sacrifice my love for the approval of this giant hermit?

Ana's thoughts seem to be on something greater. Her heart is intent on serious subjects, but now she so easily laughs and is playful. Her cheeks suddenly flush; her beautiful dark eyes wander and grow bright, as if a wave of life has been infused in her bosom. Our son is not forgotten; he is now wrapped up in this soaring love emanating from her.

This mountain is healing her and so much more. She is radiating with seductive electricity. Here, above the forests, far from the equator, love is a flame itself that transforms the night. A divine light emanates from her involuntarily, a voluptuous halo; and at the very moment when she blushes at her own beauty, she defuses her intoxicating glow of love. It is as if my eyes are opening to see Ana for the first time.

My own heart is becoming lighter. I can feel something other than a dark weight for the first time in months. My boy is there, glowing in my memory, not wrapped in black cloth and tortured by the master of death. Every good thought flourishes and creates a harvest of bliss.

This shift in manner is not exclusive to us. The written accounts from others that I share in this book all reveal an impression was made upon the soul of the climber. Precisely what influence had these mountaineers come under? They had all taken the same route to its summit. What, if anything, happened along the way that affected them so deeply? Why was I, who had not ascended the ultimate peak, changing, evolving and healing?

Dr. Clark's climbing companion, Capt. Sherwill, underwent his own changes on the mountain. Here is his account as they continue their ascent:

Ascent of Sherwill & Clark, as told

by Capt. Sherwill, 1825

"About four in the morning, my companions began to awaken and were soon on the alert. To some degree, I envied them the comfortable sleep they had experienced; such a pleasure was denied to me by the constant nausea that had not left me during the night. The thermometer marked two degrees below zero. Dr. Clark was full of beans and excited to continue, having apparently had a vivid dream last night.

Clark, an upstanding, even formal doctor gentleman, was also moody. At one moment he was engaged and lively, the next he seemed sullen. I didn't know what to expect. Though I never knew him well, overall, he seemed intensely lonely and sad and appeared to want to be left alone much of the time. It was good to see him so enthusiastic this morning as it encouraged me onward.

As soon as breakfast was finished, we made preparations for our second day's march and having determined to sleep at the same place the second night, we left a great part of our baggage. Towards five, we were all in readiness; the ropes were again affixed to us and we started forth, linked together like criminals to be tried for life or worse, death. Coutet gave us a paper bag of figs and raisins, which he said would be acceptable to munch on occasionally with a handful of snow.

On descending from the Grands Mulets, we passed by the ruins of the small hut de Saussure had erected during his visit to Mont Blanc in 1787. It was a good deal encumbered with snow and the walls did not appear more than two or three feet high. I preferred the spot we had chosen for our night's lodging, as the views were more extensive.

The sky was clear and the morning cold, although the sun had already influenced our thermometer before we left the Grands Mulets. It had risen one degree.

The Glacier de Tacconaz is not so difficult to traverse as the one we had encountered yesterday, but I should say it was more replete with beauties of its own peculiar kind. It would be endless to detail for you our progress over the crevices, our descent into them, and the difficulties of overcoming the irregularities on the ice. These glaciers, as well as others among the Alps, are in many places five hundred or six hundred feet thick. Where the inclination of the rock on which they are formed makes an angle of thirty or forty degrees, their descent seems somewhat rapid towards the valley; of course, this is imperceptible to the eye.

The ice in these lofty regions is plainly formed in a different manner from all other ice. There is a constant though gentle thaw in the day and the humidity freezes it every night. These glaciers are constantly fed; not only by the snows, but by a thousand smaller glaciers that descend from the peaks through the ravines to aid the growth of the greater.

We continued our journey across the Glacier de Tacconaz in a direction leading towards the Dôme du Goûter. In about two hours, we encountered fresh difficulties we had not experienced before from the fresh-fallen snows; the surface was frozen to the thickness of a coin, not sufficient to bear our weight. Consequently, the fatigue of walking became very great as we had now lost all solid footing.

The guides were obliged to advance a considerable distance before us in order to ascertain the most practicable path. We frequently halted some minutes for their return, and, if their report was unfavorable, we changed our direction and pursued another. The perseverance of the guides was beyond all praise.

It was towards nine that we began to feel a strong somnolence; the sensation cannot be described for it is instantaneous. While we were in movement it was less perceptible; but as soon as we remained stationary, the desire to sleep overcame us. We frequently were obliged to sit down on the snow and beg the guides for a few minutes rest.

Our thirst also became very annoying. We could only utter two or three words if we moistened our throats with snow. We had no chance of finding water in the refreshing pools and bright streams that had given us so much pleasure during our walk yesterday.

Having now reached a highly rarified air, respiration became difficult. Every fifteen or eighteen paces we were obliged to halt and turn ourselves around in the direction of the light wind so we could breathe more freely. However, as soon as we halted to breathe, sleep attacked.

During this entire day, a variety of enemies conspired to prevent our arrival at the summit of the mountain. Dr. Clark was constantly in advance and it was necessary to summon all my force and courage to keep up with him. Often, I found myself in a mechanical mode of walking and I became almost insensible from fatigue.

Numbly, for an hour, I followed as we traversed Le Petit Plateau and arrived at the foot of a second and much steeper ascent which conducts to the Grand Plateau. The desire for sleep, a burning sun on our heads, ice cold feet, shortness of breath and nausea rendered this ascent extremely fatiguing. I was sick of body and wondered if I was sick of mind as well to have done this.

On arriving at the summit of this difficult ascent, we all sat down to eat our breakfast. It was now eleven and we had hoped to be much nearer the top of Mont Blanc, but the fresh-fallen snow had impeded our progress. Even the hardy guides began to complain of fatigue. We had entirely lost our appetite and even the guides did not eat.

We drank some wine with snow, ate a small part of a fowl and remained to rest in this place for half an hour, with every hope and expectation of being on the summit of Mont Blanc in three or four hours.

I asked Coutet if I could lie down and sleep on the snow for a few minutes. He gave his consent rather reluctantly. Spreading out my coat and giving me his knapsack for a pillow, I fell back and was immediately in a profound sleep. In ten minutes, he woke me or I might have slept forever.

We had lost all sight of the peaceful and happy valley of Chamonix of which we were just yesterday the inmates. Nothing was visible but endless tracts of snow all around and a burning sun above. Not a trace of any living creature was to be found; all was silent, not a sound to disturb the solitude. I would willingly have enjoyed this extraordinary scenery still longer, but the word was given to proceed. Our unavoidable delays had derailed our plans and the fear of being caught in the dusk of the evening amidst the horrors and dangerous passes of the Glacier de Tacconaz upon our return, occasioned us to hurry on.

We had passed all crevices, caverns, and dangers of this sort, but the fatigue was not diminished. Frequently, we were obliged to change our leading guides for the simple fact of walking first through the snow caused exhaustion. To walk long without stopping was totally impracticable; respiration became very short and quick. The reverberation of the sun's rays incommoded us and the heat was considerable. It appeared to me strange to be so cold and yet, to feel the scorching of the sun's rays on my body.

When we had reached the extremity of the Grand Plateau, Coutet pointed out to us the spot where he and his brother guides were engulfed in an avalanche that fell from the very precipice we were now about to climb. We stopped for a few minutes, but were soon hurried on, lest a similar catastrophe should overtake us.

The surface of the Plateau indicated that a fall had taken place not longer than six or eight days ago. The irregularities and mountains of snow that were driven together showed very plainly that the fall had been considerable. We reckoned its extent to be nearly two miles long. Silence and expedition were imposed on us by our guides; neither of which made sense. To talk, we had little inducement and to hurry on, overcome as we were with fatigue, was next to impossible.

We now took an oblique direction, winding around a very steep ascent at the foot of the Rochers Rouges. We found this part difficult. By a zigzag movement, we left this bare granite rock on our left and arrived at a small plain which conducts to the Petits Mulets. We sat down for ten minutes to recruit our strength and drink a glass of wine to all our friends below; the guides threw off their knapsacks, and shaking each other cordially by the hand, seemed to forget all their fatigue.

I must acknowledge to you that I looked up at the magnificent summit of Mont Blanc from this point almost without consciousness. The strength and force we possess when walking through the beautiful valleys of Switzerland or Savoy are well exhausted when we arrive at the top of their stupendous mountains. The mind becomes worn down by fatigue, as well as by the changes the body must necessarily undergo in passing through these different atmospheres. Its powers are enervated almost to annihilation. However, though weary and feeble, we had no thought of abandoning our objective.

Dr. Clark and two of the guides led the way; JM Coutet and Pierre Simon. Their aid here was essential for this last ascent was icy, with scarcely any snow to prevent slipping; at the same time, so steep that the surface sometimes appeared close to your face.

The wind, as we continued to ascend, was bitterly cold. We had tied some extra handkerchiefs over our ears and chin and Coutet buttoned up closely his jacket. Simon had never been up and though his strength and spirits had not failed him, he complained and suffered a good deal from pain in his eyes.

Two or three minutes after three, we arrived at the utmost summit of Mont Blanc. I stood motionless for some time to take in a general view of this strange wild world of mountains and I could scarcely believe where I was.

We proceeded towards the center and immediately fixed three poles in a triangular form and suspended the barometer and thermometer to them.

The sun was in the southwest and interrupted our view in the direction of Geneva. On the opposite side of Mont Blanc, the Apennines were visible for a vast extent and the situations of Milan and Turin were pointed out to us. We looked very carefully and with an earnest desire, wished to see the Mediterranean Sea, but I cannot say that I saw it.

The day was remarkable—there was not a cloud above our heads; but on many of the lesser chains of mountains, and on the Apennines, there were light clouds and vapor.

Coutet endeavored to make me see a star, but either he was mistaken or his eyes were better than mine. I walked to the extreme end of the summit and looked over towards the Maritime Alps. The length of the summit of Mont Blanc is two hundred paces and nearly level. I found difficulty in measuring the width, for the sides are an immediate descent. I did not know where it began or where it finished. The whole figure may be understood by the common term, a hog's back shape. It was evident from the drifts of snow that its appearance can change in twenty-four hours.

While stationary on the summit of Mont Blanc, I experienced a very peculiar sensation of lightness of body. The rarity of the air did not affect me quite so much on the summit as when laboring through the deep snows and climbing the ascents on our passage, but now, I had the keen sensation that I was *levitating*. I rose above the summit and looked down at my companions. I laughed wickedly, loudly, my expression somehow echoing and re-echoing in the thin air.

"Can you see me?!" I shouted.

No one looked up at me though I was clearly looking down on them. I swirled above them and hovered, like a raptor, over my prey. My senses were sharp, but the faculties of my mind were in less activity. The sky was of a very dark indigo blue. This deep tint was among the most remarkable features. It looked like a dark ocean of infinite space.

Suddenly, I collapsed, feeling my body hit the granite with a bruising thud. All was black and dark, but gradually brightened. A creature of the most fantastical colors, invisible to my eye but stark in its presence, became known to me. It stroked my head, bloodying my face with its talons.

"Leave me alone!" I shrieked.

Julien yanked at me and maneuvered me to stand up, obliterating my dream. The snow was drifting from the neighboring mountains, and was hurrying along the surface of the summit about halfway up to our knees. This drifting snow, meeting with resistance, such as the body or legs of a man, would accumulate fast. Coutet recommended we leave the summit at once.

We took one more general view to fix on our minds the wonderful panorama spread before us as a sensation like no other came over me. I felt a crushing humility. How I wish everyone can be transported here without experiencing the dangers and difficulties and enjoy the magnificence of this wondrous scene.

You may imagine that any other solitude is very similar to this or that the silence of the lonely glen or dark forest can compare to the stillness up here, but you would be wrong. The wildness of the whole imposes on the mind a totally different feeling to that which we have ever experienced. There is grandeur, savageness and awfulness in these regions that seem to hurry the soul of man into a state of distraction. It renders the prospect unlike those scenes of quietude that soothe and soften the mind and bid its reflection with composure. The mountain does not care about soothing us.

I stood amidst the frowns of a savage Nature, almost insensible to every object beneath, and could see my entire life in full view. I became aware of the importance of having a purpose and opening my eyes to the raw reality of a life that is left to drift aimlessly. To have no central purpose in life is to fall easy prey to petty worries, fears, troubles, self-pity, drink or worse. I've been adrift many times; losing myself in women and alcohol. There was no lasting reward in that; I only drove myself deeper into ignorant thought, and avoidance of reality is not living. The mountain demands courage – that I face every obstacle.

In the face of this grand challenge, my thoughts turn to a more worthy train of reflection. Thoughts of injustice melt away. Pettiness is regarded as a waste of time. The dignity of humanity rises and rejoices to the ultimate abode of truth – that we are who we make ourselves to be by our thoughts and actions.

I may have achieved the mountain peak, but I was not the victor. As we began to descend Mont Blanc in a strengthening gale, I said, "Mountain, you have won."

Tears

Could Sherwill and Clark have been similar in disposition and outlook that they had both concluded the White Mountain alters the human soul? I would not call myself a religious man or even a spiritual man, but a devouring power had taken possession of me. I was eager to give it more food, particularly upon seeing all the changes in Ana.

The mountain air is still sweet in this winter climate. Every odor has its own fragrance, its own mystery, and speaks its own language; even the scent of my wife. It is voluptuous and sweet. When her mood has darkened, particularly over the mistreatment of an animal in the village, her momentary and divinely bitter fragrance mingles with the perfume of love.

She has always had these delicate sentiments. I had just forgotten them. In our years together, she never plucks a flower without regret, and in spite of herself, asks for forgiveness in doing so. Under Ana's influence, I now see how each flower has its own peculiar pretty way. Together in a bouquet, it has a special harmony, a charm it derives from Mother Earth. I now notice the graceful curves, the sweet and jaunty air with which each flower carries its pretty little head.

I know I am under a powerful, drugged influence now. Has the air of this region been tested? Do the mighty vapors of the opium plant somehow travel from the Far East and make their way here, settling in the region and drugging its victims in wave after wave of exquisite sensations of love and keen awareness of beauty?

The flame of love burns brightly within Ana and it gives me comfort and peace. All the powers of love, the warmth of her blood and her deep empathy arouse her to activity and enthusiasm. She is the most loving, the most generous and this stems from the richness of her heart. The fact that this woman is now so engaged with life, I attribute to her treasure trove of tenderness; to that ocean of goodness that permeates her heart and makes me strive to be a better human being.

Love is an idealist and when looking at one's beloved, perhaps we see only a glowing spirit. The noble and high result from cultivating a respect for each other makes our love sweet and dear to my heart. It is impossible not to surrender to this dulcitude.

For me, there has also been a radical demand for self-examination. Terrifying as it is, this systematic introspection has been as painful as it has been profoundly healing. It is as if the mountain knows my thoughts. I have successfully suppressed my doubts and fear and guilt my entire life, but now, I can no longer do that. I am confronted from moment to moment to deal with all that I have left in my wake. My missteps are not grossly divergent from the failings of most men, but still, they are my failings and to my son, they were glaring shortcomings. The awareness of this is not a passage into self-pity, but a rebirth into personal accountability.

Stan, my editor, called several days ago, asking for an update and I had mumbled some words that didn't make much sense to either him or me. My interest has shifted from the physical ascent of the mountain to the profound changes one undergoes in this region, but I didn't tell him that. I knew Stan was more interested in the ascent of the mountain than the ascent of the human soul. But which, I ask, is more important?

I turned next to the experience of John Auldjo, traveler, geologist, writer, Deputy Grand Master of Upper Canada and later, British Consul at Geneva, who documented his August 1827 ascent of Mont Blanc as follows:

Ascent of John Auldjo, 1827

"It was on passing the beautiful little Lake Chede on my way to Chamonix, early in

June, that the "monarch of the Alps" first presented himself to me in that dazzling splendor with which he is clothed. His blanched head, far above the thick robe of clouds that envelop his center, reflected the brilliancy of the noon-day sun. The mind, at first lost in astonishment, and gradually recovering from its effects, dwells with admiration on the magnificent scene. The beholder then feels an earnest desire to reach the summit, though epically difficult and dangerous.

It was at this moment that I formed the determination to attempt the ascent of Mont Blanc. The desire of exploring the glaciers of Bossons and Taconnaz was not diminished nor the resolution of proceeding to the summit of the mountain by the frowning precipices, their lofty pyramids of azure and the dazzling glare of their snows. They only excited my impatience to realize the arduous undertaking. But the season was not sufficiently advanced, and no guide would accompany me until the end of July. I left Chamonix with regret, but with a determination to return. This desire I could not shake in the weeks that followed. I had not desired anything, human or material, more than the ascent of Mont Blanc. I anxiously waited for word.

Finally, on the 5th of August 1827, I arrived in the valley. For several weeks, the weather had been beautiful, during which period not a cloud had sullied the blue arch of heaven, nor a mist shrouded the bright horizon. This day, however, the clouds gathered thick and glowering and rain fell in torrents, pouring down a deluge the whole afternoon and the ensuing night.

The next morning, the mountain I was about to climb was no longer visible. It was closely wrapped in a veil of dark vapor. The wind blew with great violence, sweeping through this narrow valley in awful gusts. The weather wore a threatening and stormy appearance. I was angry, anxious and frustrated by its temptation and teasing of me these long months only to check my desire now.

Even the guides seemed to despair and almost concluded that it would be too dangerous to encounter the glacier. They estimated an attempt in ten or fourteen days, but by then it might be too far advanced in the season for an undertaking. However inconvenient and unpleasant it was to remain in Chamonix for that period, I was determined to do so. I wanted to be ready to go as soon as the first favorable change in the weather. I did not allow myself to be depressed. I imagined the beauties of the glaciers over which I would pass. Above all, the anticipation of the pleasure that I would derive from a successful ascent produced in my mind an animated excitement. The constant change of visitors to the valley also distracted me and provided a great source of amusement. It was hardly possible for ennui.

One early Tuesday morning, Julien Devouassoux and JM Coutet entered my chamber and announced that the wind had changed, the weather was fine and if it lasted the day, it would most certainly continue the following day.

In these mountainous districts, the guides are very good barometers and seldom give a wrong indication of the approaching weather. With great joy, I heard them say that we would start the next morning. It was most gratifying to me, having been led to expect a ten-day wait in the valley.

Many of the guides who had desired to be chosen, in the event we could ascend, now declined to proceed with me. The lead guide fixed three o'clock as the deadline for enrolling those who would volunteer. When that hour came, I could not fill up my list of six. Many had the excuse that their wives would not allow them to go; others said that their mothers, sisters or children interfered. I could only find four who were determined to accompany me.

In the evening, I made up the number, but again two of them changed their minds. At ten o'clock, finally, I had my six guides and was certain we would be setting off in the morning.

Two young men of the village, one a naturalist, Michel Carrier, aged 30; the other a guide's apprentice, Auguste Couttet, aged 19, strenuously begged to be allowed to join my party. They were both led by curiosity, and finding that the guides were not averse to their accompanying us, I granted permission. My six guides were as follows:

1. JM Coutet, married, aged 37; had been up seven times; was nearly killed by the avalanche in Dr. Hamel's attempt. He was my chief guide, and in very dangerous places always took the lead.

2. Julien Devouassoux, married, aged 38; up once; was one of Dr. Hamel's guides; saved Coutet, being precipitated into a crevice with him. His duty was to remain attached to my person. In his prudence and presence of mind I firmly relied. His bravery is well known.

3. Jean Pierre Tairraz, up twice; aged 40; single.

4. Jacques Simond, married, aged 40; never up.

5. Michel Favret, widower, aged 31; up once.

6. Jean-Marie Coutet, married, aged 49; never up.

Six in the morning was the time fixed for starting and every man said he would be in attendance before that hour, but they did not arrive on time. Four had to part from their wives and children; some crying, some upbraiding me. Many a bitter tear flowed and more than one heart waxed heavy that morning.

Two or three of my countrymen were kind enough to accompany me through the weeping crowd assembled on the bridge. One carried his attention so far as to continue with me to Coutet's cottage, the appointed rendezvous. Coutet was dressed in an old hussar jacket with a scarlet embroidered vest; the uniform he wore while serving in the French army. Apparently, the uniform is only worn now on an expedition up Mont Blanc. He also brought out a number of straw hats with broad brims, all celebrated for having been more than once on the summit. He presented them to me, so I may choose one to wear.

We left the village at seven and immediately began to ascend through the thick pine wood which surrounds the cottages. Among the trees we occasionally observed groups of females parting from their friends. After an ascent of an hour and a half up the mountain, which is bounded on one side by the Glacier de Bossons, and on the other by the ravine through which the torrent flows, we arrived at the Chalet de la Para, a summer chalet belonging to the old guide Favret, and the last inhabited spot on the mountain. From this, we ascended a steep path for about an hour, and arrived at the Pierre Pointue, where I was obliged to leave the mule which I had ridden thus far.

It was near mid-day and I was anxious to get in good time to the Grands Mulets. I hurried the guides, who were dividing wood and squabbling in good humor, each desirous of getting as light a burden as possible. One or two of the guides had employed others to carry their loads and paid very dearly for this indulgence to save their own shoulders.

At twenty minutes before twelve, we left this station and ascending a little further, arrived at the edge of the glacier. We had not much difficulty in getting on it, but to an inexperienced eye it would seem impossible to proceed any great distance from the masses of ice that were piled on one another and the deep and wide fissures.

An extended plain of snow now presented itself here and there covered with masses of broken ice. Sometimes a beautiful tower raised its blue form and seemed to mock the lofty pointed rocks above it. It looked like a castle on whose dilapidated walls the ivy, hanging in clustering beauty, or lying in rich and dark luxuriance, was, by the wand of some fairy, changed into the bright matter which now composed it.

From these magnificent scenes and over this plain, we hurried as speedily as circumstances would allow to avoid those dangerous avalanches that fall continually from the Aiguille du Midi. The pyramids of ice that rose on either side of us, in all the sublime variety of nature, forming a thousand different shapes, kept me riveted to the spot. As they increased in number and size, I became lost in admiration, unwilling to leave them and move forward, until the voice of a guide exhorted me. Extraordinarily, he led the way over places where one would believe it impossible for a human foot to tread. We passed among the remains of innumerable avalanches that had been long accumulating and formed a most uneven and tiresome footway.

It was the avalanche alone we feared, but now new dangers arose from the crevices, those deep clefts in the ice formed by the constant movement of the main body that separates immense parts of it. The higher masses, meeting with slight opposition, remain stationary; the lower, proceeding in their course, widen the breach and throughout the whole glacier, in every direction, form tremendous cracks.

Here, we rested ten minutes in arranging the line and adjusting the cords. The first two guides were tied together at a distance of six yards; the third and fourth in like manner; then myself. The rope was fastened around my chest, each end being tied to a guide; Coutet leading, and Devouassoux being behind me; the naturalist and the boy followed, also secured together.

No men could be in higher spirits than my guides, who were laughing, singing and joking, but when we came to dangerous passes, the grave, serious look took the place of the smiling countenance. The moment we were safely by it, the smile returned and everyone vied in giving amusement to the other. These were situations in which the nerves were put to a severe test. However stout the heart may be, if giddiness should take possession of the brain, the most determined courage would be of little avail. It is exceedingly difficult to look into these depths which must be passed over and not be unnerved; knowing that if the head fails, destruction is inevitable.

I was unaccustomed to look into such danger, but found my head could bear it and with a steady eye, I saw only a beautiful abyss. I was dizzy with its stunning attraction. I felt this urge to plunge into its depth and revel in its icy snare, but my guides broke my trance by expressing their fears that I could yield to fatigue.

I believe my strong determination to reach the summit was of more service to me than all the physical preparations. I was bonded to this scene and enlivened on its slope. I did all I could to contain my desire to abandon the party and be alone with it. I was experiencing such strange fancies and desires of being one with the mountain.

As we trekked on, a large mass of ice opposed our progress. We passed it by climbing up its glassy sides. After winding for some time among chasms and enormous towers, we arrived at the edge of another crevice, over which we could see one bridge; not of ice, but of snow and so thin that it was deemed impossible to trust to it. A plan was resorted to enable us to pass over in safety. Our batons were placed on it and in doing so, the center gave way and fell into the gulf. However, enough remained on each side to form a narrow bridge, requiring great precaution and steadiness to traverse. Other crevices were passed over; bridges of snow too weak to walk on or too extended to admit this application of the poles. A strong guide managed to creep over and with a rope tied around the waist of a second (who then lay on his back) he was then pulled across by the first guide. In this manner, the whole party was drawn over the crevice. The snow was generally soft so that my head and shoulders plowed a furrow as I was dragged through it. My body was covered in this powdery splendor and the contact was profoundly titillating. The passage of these bridges, though difficult and dangerous, also excited the rest of the party and a strange loud laugh accompanied each man as he was jerked over the gulf yawning beneath him.

Again the glacier presented its beautiful and varied scenes; every moment it mesmerized my eye in its icy grandeur and I had to be urged on by others in order to move. The crevices, numerous and deep, broken and full of hollows or caves, surpassed anything I could have conceived. Some of these grottoes were accessible; others were blocked up by pillars studded with ornaments of ice or snow that could only be examined externally. We entered one so beautiful in construction and embellishments, that it could have been called the "spirit of the mountain." It was large, its roof supported by thick icicles of blue or white varying in a thousand different shades. On the floor were vast clumps of ice that resembled crystal flowers; formed by the freezing of drops of water that are perpetually falling. In the center, a pool of water stood in its blue basin. The refreshing coolness and exquisite clearness excited my thirst. At the further end fell a cascade into a sort of spiral and in its passage produced a sound much like that of water boiling in a confined vessel.

The guides are the many lovers that pass through these ice temples. They plunge into the ice and snow and find release upon its banks. They service it and it services them. The wives and lovers are no match. The mountain always wins. Sooner or later, men leave the bed of their lovers to ascend the greatest passion of their lives. The tears and cries and pleas of others will never ring louder than the call of the mountain. It took immense inner strength for me to leave this sacred cathedral.

Arriving near the base of the Grands Mulets, we found that a chasm of eighty feet in width separated it from us. No time was to be lost. We were standing in a very perilous situation. JM Coutet commenced cutting steps on the angle with his hatchet and after great labor and considerable danger, he got to the top and was immediately followed by another guide. The knapsacks were then drawn up and the rest of the party after them. In ascending this wall, being partly drawn up, partly clambering, I stopped for an instant and looked down into the abyss beneath me. The blood curdled in my veins as I had never beheld anything so terrific. The great beauty of the immense crevices around us, so deep and so bright, excited not only my admiration, but even that of the guides, accustomed as they were to such scenes. We were spellbound, dangling there, keenly alive and yet fascinated with an icy death. We had to shout at each other to break the trance.

Safely on the top and looking around, we discovered that these large crevices extended on each side at a great distance. The plane of the wall, sloped from the upper to the lower crevice with an inclination, rendered walking on it very perilous. As the space became wider, I became less cautious and while looking over the edge into the upper crevice, my feet slid out from under me. I came down on my face and glided rapidly towards the lower one. I cried out, but the guides who held the ropes attached to me did not stop me. They stood firm. I got to the extent of the rope; my feet hanging over the lower crevice, one hand grasping firmly the pole, and the other my hat. The guides yelled for me to be cool and unafraid. It was a difficult time to be cool, hanging over an abyss, and in momentary expectation of falling into it! They made no attempt to pull me up for some time, but told me to raise myself on the rope. This had all been designed to check the fall of everyone.

I was shaken, but still with presence of mind to continue. Marching at an angle of 45 degrees with the crevice, we approached the rock. Another fissure was in our way. The lead guide plunged his baton into the bridge of snow; then continued one step at a time, but his pole slipped from his hand and fell through the snow into the gulf beneath. He only had time to spring back on the ice, when the whole bridge sunk into the abyss. The pole bounded from side to side of the crevice and then disappeared. The poor fellow was very distressed and many plans were formed for its recovery, but none were deemed practicable as the crevice was too deep. We left the spot and soon, finding another bridge, crossed it and attained the rock near the summit of what was to be our resting place for the night.

I immediately scrambled to the summit of that area and raised a red handkerchief to signal our friends in Chamonix of our safe arrival. It was exactly four o'clock and the labors of the day now terminated, we proceeded to make arrangements for the comfort of the night. A fire was lit, some wine was warmed and distributed and a change of apparel was found extremely refreshing.

The sun, now about to set, was tinged with a purple of the softest hue and lit the whole scene below us. It gradually deepened into a beautiful crimson and shaded everything with its color. The Jura seemed on fire and the lake of Geneva reflected the glow. As the sun retired from the world beneath us, the hue shed its departing rays and then wore a dull grey. The lake and the lower mountains were soon hidden in darkness, but the summit of the mountain was still burnished with a line of bright gold. It died away slowly, leaving a bright lovely red that dwindled into the somber shade that all the world around was enveloped. The sky was now clear and deeply azure and it was getting cold (the thermometer had descended to 45 degrees Fahrenheit).

As we were to be early risers, I was not reluctant in preparing for my stony bed. I had the first place, Devouassoux next to me and the rest of the guides, in a row alongside each other, lay as close as they could to preserve warmth. I soon fell asleep, although the thunder of the falling avalanches might well have kept me awake.

In the middle of the night I awoke, but experienced none of the unpleasant nausea and sickness which had attacked others. A solitude and stillness prevailed that affected me more than any of the occurrences of the day. I felt an urgent need to sob. I am not a man who can ever recall having cried before in my life, but now I desperately wanted release from the strong emotions coursing through my body. None of the beauty and none of the danger made a more lasting impression upon me than the awful silence of that night; broken only by the loud crash of falling ice, echoing and re-echoing with a thrilling sound in the death-like stillness.

The sky had become more darkly blue and the moon shone in the softest brightness; the stars shed a dazzling and brilliant luster. The avalanches continued falling, but neither they, nor the reflection on the past day, nor the anxieties for the coming one, could keep me from the effects of fatigue. I looked at my companions all sound asleep. They slept so placidly, yet I longed to get out of the tent, to behold the wonderful scenery under the influence of the moonlight and scream out all of these contained emotions. However, I could not have done so without waking every one of my dormant guides and I was unwilling to sacrifice their sleep for this gratification. I lay down and it was not long before I participated in the sound slumber they enjoyed. I dreamed of a woman with the softness curves and the deepest crevices and the sweetest scent. She was all too real and I experienced exquisite release with her.

I was startled suddenly and saw Julien creeping into the tent. I didn't want to leave my stony bed, but he urged me to get up. I examined the thermometer. The mercury was at 35 degrees

Fahrenheit. The sheet that formed our tent had been moistened by the heat from within and in the course of the night, had frozen.

The moon was shining with great brilliancy. The effect of its light upon the snow and glaciers was beautiful and soft. The stars seemed to be suspended far beneath the ethereal canopy and shone without scintillation. The appearance of Mont Blanc was particularly grand and sublime; the deep indigo color of the sky formed a strong contrast with the silvery brightness of the snow. The whole scene was of a deeply impressive nature.

It was excessively cold and I felt it, even though I had taken every possible precaution in the way of clothing and fur gloves to resist its force. Leaving part of the provisions, knapsacks, and clothes, which we had changed the night before, we started from the tent at half past three in the morning, and soon descended to the ice, which was so hard that it received no impression from our steps. We endeavored to get warm by the exertion of walking as fast as was consistent with the caution required in stepping on ice, but the attempt was in vain. The cold was piercing, the snow collected on our shoes congealed and severely affected our feet; while the whole frame was pervaded by a sense of pain from the intense cold.

We now directed our course towards the Dôme du Goûter, walking obliquely up a gently inclined hill and then arrived at a very steep mound of snow, up which we proceeded in a zigzag direction until we reached the top. So slippery and hard was the ice that we found it necessary to cut deep steps in it. The pain that we experienced from the cold was greatly aggravated by waiting. During these pauses, nothing broke upon the profound silence of the vast and chilling solitude, but the crash of the heavy stroke of the axe. It was then that I gazed around and took in the wondrous and appalling spectacle. It filled my mind with awe and penetrated my soul. I felt dizzy, sick and overwhelmed by an internal hunger that had nothing to do with food.

My attention was now attracted by the sun rising. The rays were falling on Mont Blanc and the Dôme du Goûter, clothing them in a variety of brilliant colors, quickly following one another from a light tint of crimson to rich purple and then to bright gold. These rapid alternations of reflected splendor on a surface so vast and sublimely picturesque presented a scene of dazzling brilliance that was almost too much to bear.

From this plain, we ascended a long steep hill, so steep that following each other in the zigzag direction in which we were obliged to climb, my head was generally on a line with the knee of the guide just before me. It was fatiguing and dreadfully cold. In fact, so tedious was our progress in ascending these peaks of ice, that we all felt exhausted, particularly as we had taken no refreshment since we started in the morning.

At last, we attained the Grand Plateau. The sun was shining on some parts of the Plateau, but far from us. As we all felt the bitter cold, we agreed to stop at the commencement of the plain in a crevice of from fifteen to twenty feet in width. In it, we found a bridge of snow that was considered strong enough to bear the whole party. From its position in the chasm, it afforded shelter from the north wind. We, therefore, chose this bridge to breakfast upon. It was past seven and we had been walking for more than four hours without any cessation, but the wearying and tedious halting. It was with pleasure that I found myself resting in this comfortable crevice.

While breakfast was in preparation, I could not resist the temptation of wandering along the edge of the crevice on the Plateau side. The depth of it was immense; its great breadth afforded me an opportunity of making a more accurate and perfect examination than I had before. The layers of ice forming the glacier, varying in color from deep bluish-green to a silvery whiteness with myriads of long clear icicles hanging from all the little breaks in the strata, presented a scene of the greatest beauty.

From this point, I had a view of the bridge with all the guides sitting on it. Beneath them was a stupendous chasm. In one moment, without a chance for escape, the fall of the bridge would plunge them all into the gulf beneath. Yet no such idea seemed to enter the imagination of my thoughtless, but brave guides. They sat there singing and laughing, either unconscious to or despite the danger. Observing this in the abstract, I would have wondered what had taken possession of them, but my own experience of the mountain had taught me how well it charms and deceives.

After our rest, we traversed the Plateau, winding towards the left; leaving the old route that led right across the plain, and up the steep masses of snow and ice that hang on this side of Mont Blanc. So delicately and dangerously poised is this, that the slightest noise or concussion of the air, even from speaking, can move them from their situation and then they fall, rushing down the declivities with overwhelming velocity, widening as they proceed, until at last they extend from one side of the mountain to the other and cover the plain below with debris.

At last, the sun shone upon us with animating heat, and welcome it was, for our pace was too steady and slow to give us an opportunity of keeping ourselves warm by exercise. Cold and numb as we were, we could hardly have borne the fatigue we now had to undertake. It was only small consolation that we knew it was going to be our last severe trial to the summit. Here, in the rarified air with the fatigue arising from climbing the almost perpendicular ascent which leads directly to the summit, I nearly wanted to quit. That awful sobbing sensation came over me again, but my fear of this last trial soon set me straight.

The approach to this last danger was from the Plateau. We had to first descend to a ledge projecting from the side of a wide crevice, and hanging over an abyss. It was a wedge of ice, covered with frozen snow, propped like a buttress against a perpendicular precipice of the glacier; the face of which rose a few feet above the termination of the slope. Having scaled this part of it, we found a declivity of snow, inclining towards the precipice at an angle of about 50 degrees. Turning to our left, we were obliged to walk along the edge of this precipice for some minutes, and then in a zigzag to ascend the hill until we came to a plain. Having accomplished this, our success was now considered quite certain, and we congratulated each other on this happy circumstance, which inspired each member of the party with fresh animation and spirit.

While engaged in passing this last difficulty, our attention was arrested by a loud noise, or hissing sound, which the guides knew to proceed from a vast body of ice and snow falling in avalanche. It lasted some moments and finished by a report that must have been caused by the precipitation of some immense mass upon a rock or plain. In an instant, the awful calm that had been disturbed, resumed its reign.

A slightly-inclined plain of snow, presenting no difficulty, allowed us to quicken our pace, and proceed with more comfort. The pain that we suffered from the cold had become acute, producing a shivering throughout the limbs too great to be much longer endured, and which nothing but the increased rapidity of our march could alleviate.

An ascent of snow rose between us and the summit of the Rochers Rouges. It was here that I felt the first symptoms of the effect produced on the body by the rarity of the air. I was seized with an oppression of the chest and a slight difficulty of breathing. A quickness of pulse soon followed with a palpitation of the heart, a great inclination of thirst, and a fullness in the veins of my head, but still I experienced no headache.

We crossed a plain of snow which rose gently from the Rochers Rouges; at the end of it was the only crevice we had met for some time: it was deep and wide. One bridge was tried, but it gave way; a little further another was found, over which we managed to pass by being drawn across on our backs. Two or three managed to walk across another, using great care, but, when we had proceeded some little distance up the acclivity before us, we were surprised by a shrill scream. Turning around, we saw the youngster, Jean-Marie Coutet, had fallen up to his arms. The perilous situation he was in was appalling. We all ran down to him and he was drawn out, but he had nearly lost his mind. He was terrified. However, he soon recovered, and acknowledged his lack of precaution and focus.

The ascent from this point was very steep and the difficulty of surmounting it was greatly increased; the rarity of the atmosphere became exceedingly oppressive. I was attacked with a pain in my head; intense thirst; the difficulty of breathing much greater. The new symptoms I now experienced were violent palpitations of the heart, a general lassitude of the frame and a very distressing sensation of pain in the knees and muscles of the thighs that I was scarcely able to move them.

On reaching these rocks, I was so exhausted that I wished to sleep, but the experienced guides would not permit it. From the Rochers Rouges, we saw that there were many people on the Brevent watching our progress; among them we recognized some female forms. The discovery of female spectators renewed our courage and excited us to greater efforts than before.

Although the sun was shining on us, I felt extremely cold on one side of my body in the cutting blast. The other side of my body was being warmed by the sun but it increased the shivering. My shoes and gaiters were frozen hard and my feet were numb. Some of the guides were also similarly affected and even suffered more than myself, but all were anxious to get on; evincing a resolute determination that was quite wonderful in the state they were in.

I became passive and limp as two of the least exhausted guides forced me up some short distance, each taking an arm. They soon devised a plan less strenuous to them. While I rested, lying down at full length, two of them went up in advance about fourteen paces and fixed themselves on the snow; a long rope was fastened around my chest and the other end to them. I was able to stand and move my legs. They pulled me towards them so that I was partly drawn up and partly running up using a zigzag direction. The amusement derived from this process must have delighted the observers on Brevent. They were rewarding us by waving their hats and handkerchiefs. I could also just distinguish the people in Chamonix collected in considerable numbers on the bridge, watching our progress and success as we finally reached the summit of Mont Blanc. It was exactly eleven o'clock.

The wind blew with considerable force. I was too worn out to remain there long or to examine the scene around me. The sun shone brilliantly on every peak of snow that I could see. Hardly any mist hung over the valleys; none was on the mountains. The object of my ambition and my toil had been gained, but I flung myself into the snow in a sheltered area and was soundly asleep within seconds.

In this state, I remained for fifteen minutes. When I was roused to survey the mighty picture beneath, I found myself much relieved, but still had a slight shivering. The pain in my legs had ceased, as well as the headache, but the thirst remained. My pulse was very quick and the difficulty of breathing great, but not as oppressive as it had been.

I went to the highest point to observe my friends on the Brevent and in Chamonix once more, but was summoned by the guides to eat. We consumed bread and roasted chicken, but I could not swallow the slightest morsel. Even the smell of the food created nausea.

The most peculiar sensation was the awful stillness that continued to reign; unbroken by human voices. It weighed deeply upon my mind with a power that is impossible to describe. I have never seen anything that could exceed the singular and splendid appearance the sky and the sun presented. I experienced a lightness of body, as if I could simply spread my arms and fly. In fact, I was *convinced* I could fly, but Julien was mindful to keep my feet on the granite.

Gathering my thoughts, I sat down to write a letter to my sister:

My dear Annie, It may give you some pleasure to know that I am looking down upon you at this moment. You can judge the gratification I have in being above the habitable world - a thing I've much desired. I have just drunk a bottle of wine to your health; my guides join me and we all wish you well while drinking long life and happiness, and even this high, I am not forgetful of the many times I have written and now write again that I am your affectionate brother, John.

The guides all signed the back of the letter and we determined the descent to Chamonix was necessary to begin. The ropes were therefore adjusted and other preparations made for starting the descent. Whatever reluctance I might have felt in the middle part of our ascent from the Grands Mulets, the stupendous scene around me exceeded my expectations. I was capable of appreciating its beauty and wonder and there did not seem as if anything at the base of the mountain or elsewhere in the world could be as rewarding as being on this summit.

Urged to begin the descent, I tore myself away from this place like no other on Earth. The emotions came roaring up through me. I clasped my face and wept for the first time in my life."

Passion

Like John Auldjo, our own emotions are difficult to contain in this mountain air. Thoughts and fears of death disappeared in my profound absorption with the mountain. Whether at its feet or on its mid-slope, I became completely obsessed with the belief that Mont Blanc was as aware of me as I was aware of it.

The mountain gave me a keen appreciation for Mother Earth. In this elastic atmosphere, I felt her very plainly caressing and pitying, healing and warming me, her wounded child, outside my body and within my body. Her forces interpenetrated my frame with her vivifying principles and insinuated into my being her very soul. The identification between us grew complete. I could no longer distinguish myself from Earth.

You may scoff or even laugh at this notion, but you are not here. You have not been over-taken by the forces of Mont Blanc and its profound relationship with Earth. Until you experience this, you have not truly lived.

It was like the perfect marriage, more than a marriage, between me and Earth. More fittingly, I could describe it as "an exchange of nature." I was Earth and she was human. She had taken all of me upon her shoulders while I, in becoming Earth, had assumed her life, warmth and youth. Years of labor and anxiety fell to the wayside. Grief melted away. An indescribable unctuous gleam shot through my body. I was completely renewed.

Formerly, in my blind ambition and fierce toil, I had forgotten Nature and I had nearly missed true happiness until she overwhelmed me with her great apostle, Mont Blanc. In this region, with infinite gentleness, she opened her arms to me; entered into and blended with me. She filled me with life and power. I surrendered to her ample forces and with a more prolific heart, I joined with her in sacred unity.

Under this powerful influence, Ana and I became one; encapsulated and cocooned, love upon love, passion upon passion, body upon body, sharing, intermingling, craving, resisting, releasing, exploring, exploding and surrendering deeper than death but lighter than air and on that winged dream, we arrived at the metaphorical peak, where we remain.

Is Mont Blanc male? Is it female? Simply, it is everything. Once it has penetrated your consciousness, it stirs an awakening and denies sleep. It shudders, shakes and thunders its attractors from

138

slumber by whispering, "*Take me*" and that desire, want and passion remains.

Had Balmat, de Saussure and all the others come under this transformative influence of the mountain? I can only imagine their true experience and how it would punish those who turn away from all its goodness to chase after bad.

Jealousy

Jacques Balmat had been honored by the nickname "Monsieur Mont Blanc" for being the first to successfully ascend the peak. He would return again to the mountain, however, now he was more interested in plundering minerals from it. Compelled by various factors, he planned an ascent in September of 1834.

During that same September of 1834, there were more lovers of the mountain who attempted to scale Mont Blanc. Martin Barry, a British physician who studied histology and embryology and later published work on his discovery that spermatozoa could sometimes be found inside the ovum, was one of Mont Blanc's attractors. He shares his account as follows:

Ascent of Martin Barry, 1834

"As we reached the Col de Balme, on the 15th of September, in passing from Martigny to the Priory of Chamonix, Mont Blanc presented itself for the first time. It came suddenly and magnificently into view. Though inferior to Chimborazo in the Andes in its elevation above the sea, Mont Blanc is considered the higher mountain of the two as it rises 12,300 feet above the valley of Chamonix. Chimborazo is not more than 11,600 feet above the plain of Quito.

There is another important feature in Mont Blanc. Its line of perpetual snow is nearly 7,000 feet below the summit. Chimborazo's is only 2,400 feet, according to the explorer Humboldt.

With six guides, I set out the next morning, (September 16th) at eight-thirty. The enterprise became speedily and generally known in the village and, in consequence, a number of people assembled to witness our departure. The cottagers too, as we passed through the valley, gave us their best wishes. Here and there an anxious face spoke of the relationship with some of the guides.

We passed through the pine wood east of the Bossons Glacier, successively reaching the Chalet de la Para (the last human habitation), Pierre Pointue and were at Pierre al'Echelle by 12 noon. Several chamois were now seen bounding fleetly over the rocks just above us. We dined at that spot and soon afterwards, at the foot of the Aiguille du Midi, entered upon the ice, 7,000 feet in perpendicular altitude. The soles of my shoes were armed with steel points to prevent slipping. Crossing the Glacier de Bossons and obliquely ascending, we proceeded in a southwest direction towards the Grands Mulets. We hoped to pass the night there.

The great pioneers of this ascent, Coutet and Balmat, had the greatest coolness, intrepidity, experience and judgment. Of these brave men, I cannot speak too highly. Coutet was my principal guide and had been up eight times before. He was a remarkably intelligent man and I was glad to have him near me. His decisions put my entire life in his hands.

Having gained on the Grands Mulets at a point much lower down than usual, we had to get up to that area as it was to be our resting place for the night. It was a narrow ledge, but it was out of reach from avalanches. We reached this spot by six-thirty. It was a flat surface of a few square feet, forming an open shelf on the southwest side of the rock. Its margin was a precipice. Our batons, inclined against the rock, served as rafters for the roof of a little cabin we made with canvas. Two or three blankets were spread on its floor. It was 45 degrees Fahrenheit.

A fire was made a short distance from the tent and we had supper with good appetites around it. By nine o'clock, having tripled some parts of our clothing, particularly for our feet, we crept into our cabin and soon found that lying very closely together, we were sufficiently warm.

I awakened at midnight. I got up and regretted seeing that two of the guides, Coutet and Tairraz, were lying in the open air. There was not enough room in the makeshift tent. The cold, however, was not intense. It was 42 degrees Fahrenheit. A cold breeze from the southwest had entirely subsided.

It was a brilliant night. The full moon had risen over the summit of the mountain and was shining resplendent on the glazed surface of the snow. The guides were sleeping as I moved towards the precipice. We were at an elevation of ten thousand feet. Below me, in the eerie light of the moon, lay piled up the colossal masses of ice we had been climbing and whose dangers we had narrowly escaped. Around and above me was a sea of fair, but treacherous snow whose hidden perils we had yet to encounter. The Jura Mountains and many unknown peaks of Switzerland were seen dimly in the distance. Chamonix was sleeping at the foot of the mountain. Broken by the occasional thunder of an avalanche, the profoundest silence reigned. It was the vastest, sternest and most sublime image of Nature reposing. It began for me as a fitful dream then sunk me into the stillest calm. The scene held me for over an hour and a half. I was possessed by it. Finally, able to recall the coming day's fatigue, I went back to sleep.

At five in the morning of the 17th of September 1834, we left the Grands Mulets. Proceeding at first across the icy valley that lay between us and the Dôme du Goûter, we reached almost the base of the latter and then ascending more directly, often by a zigzag course, arrived at the Grand Plateau by nine o'clock.

The newly fallen snow, from a foot to eighteen inches in depth, had rendered the way fatiguing. It had been necessary for our leader to ascertain the safety of every step with the baton. We proceeded in a line, united, two or three together, with cords, following carefully the same track. Our way lay over vast fields of snow, but the early part of it had presented scenery even more magnificent than I had seen in the early morning hours at our encampment.

Chasms of unfathomable depth, great towers of ice, caverns and grottoes whose crystal walls were adorned with a tapestry of inimitable beauty were hung with a silver fringe. Such scenes live in my memory, but I can't adequately describe it in words. I felt in the depth of my soul that I never wanted to leave.

Very different feelings soon took the place of admiration for the scenery because difficulties occurred. Four years had elapsed since Mont Blanc was last ascended so we knew that changes had occurred sufficient enough to entirely prevent our further progress. The half-French, half-Italian guides I scarcely understood, but their disappointment was obvious. Their faces convinced me that the undertaking was not far from being abandoned.

A way was found to continue and we now climbed only with hope. Depressed we were on that slow and painful zigzag course. This effect was not without its physiological interest, but that gave me little comfort.

The weary ascent of this part accomplished, a great fissure next presented itself. The passage was impossible. From this point, we would have returned, except for a bridge of ice discovered at a distance. We made for it and our hopes brightened, but now we had to pass some very treacherous ice. Many holes were covered with recent snow and the dangers of the track were concealed. The lead guide repeatedly turned to warn us of openings in the ice.

How cheering, in the midst of these dangers and toils, was it to hear the voice of one of the guides shouting that we could now be seen by observers in the valley. He knew there would be observers watching our progress and I well knew that among the most anxious of them was a near relative of mine whose painful suspense during my absence had somewhat marred the pleasure of the enterprise for me. We soon afterwards reached the Grand Plateau and as the difficulties that lay before us were not too harsh, we sat down to breakfast in very good spirits and good weather.

We left the Grand Plateau before ten o'clock. Great dryness of the skin was now observed, thirst became intense and it seemed scarcely possible to alleviate it even though we were constantly eating snow. The guides had stored their pockets with sugar and French plums which were refreshing.

Our progress after leaving the Grand Plateau, at first obstructed by the passage of some very formidable cliffs of ice, had latterly been impeded only by the depth of the soft snow. Now we reached the foot of a declivity of thirty-five to forty degrees with the horizon and many hundred feet in height. It was the "right shoulder" of the summit. The snow here had hardened sufficiently to prevent our advancing a single step without holes being first cut with the hatchet. When we had reached a considerable height in the declivity, this became exceedingly dangerous.

This ascent brought us above the Rochers Rouges. The next slope was to take us to the summit, but we had now reached an elevation where the atmosphere's density was exceedingly reduced. I had not felt that until this point. Only a few steps could now be taken at a time and these became both fewer and slower. Two or three deep breaths appeared sufficient at each pause to enable me to proceed; but, on making the attempt, I found the exhaustion return. I also felt a degree of indifference even within sight of the summit. Slight faintness came on and I wanted to cry and scream, but nothing came out of my mouth. I sat down for a few minutes. After drinking a little wine, one more effort was made.

At a quarter past two, we finally stood on the highest summit, cheered on by friends and family in the valley. The exhaustion, faintness and indifference ceased. The dangers of the descent were not for a moment considered. It was with a thrill of exultation never felt before that I contemplated the stupendous splendor that is as impossible to conceive as it is to describe. The blackish-blue color of the sky, particularly in and near the zenith, was seen from this lofty region. The depth of this color is known to depend on specific causes, but the tint appeared to me to derive additional depth from the simultaneous reception of rays from the snow. Had the rarefied air presented a fantasy before my eyes or was this indeed an accurate portrayal of the summit?

The descent on the whole was very rapid. The guides were sometimes sliding down fields of snow, supported by their batons. Human forms were soon afterwards seen on the rocks below us and I had the satisfaction, truly not a small one, of recognizing among them my relative. He, as well as other observers, had witnessed our arrival on the summit and had seen us on different parts of the snowy track.

It was very interesting to me, just before reaching the valley, to meet Jacques Balmat, now seventy-two years old. He recounted his tale of danger half a century ago of a night spent in solitude in a storm, upon the glacier and of the exultation he felt when the summit was attained for the first time by the result of his own perseverance.

I was a bit uncomfortable because Balmat seemed electrified with envy of our successful ascent. We shared competing stories that made me feel like we were old friends. It was with regret that we bid each other farewell. I did not then realize how profound our parting would be."

Greed

Giving credence to vague rumors that a rich vein of gold existed on the side of one of the high peaks or perhaps in response to the victorious ascent of the Martin Barry climbing party, Balmat once again was determined to ascend Mont Blanc that September of 1834.

Balmat arrived near the spot where the gold was rumored to be, but found it inaccessible. It was necessary to traverse a narrow ledge of rock, overhanging a frightful precipice. The sight of the danger daunted him and for the moment he abandoned the attempt.

Sometime afterwards, having obtained the assistance of an intrepid chamois hunter, Balmat returned to the area and despite the prayers and expostulations of his comrade, persisted. The fascination was too strong for him. He ventured upon the narrow ledge, took several steps and then suddenly disappeared. The hunter, horrified and in despair, returned alone. Balmat's death must have been instantaneous.

Imagine a fall of more than 400 feet into an abyss filled with masses of jagged rock where avalanches continually fall. What a horrible tomb in which Balmat fell.

The details of the accident were unknown at first in Chamonix. Balmat's companion appeared to be hiding the truth so that suspicion wouldn't fall upon him. Some shepherds later claimed to have seen Balmat disappear, but also kept silent for various reasons.

The sons of Balmat made several fruitless attempts to recover their father's body. The information they were able to acquire was meager and even if they had more reliable intelligence to go upon, they could never have succeeded in raising their father's body out of the profound abyss.

Nineteen years rolled by without anyone thinking of undertaking fresh searches. The frightful description that was given of the abyss and the dangers that must be encountered deterred the bravest hearts. Unfortunate Balmat, if he was there, was to remain lying at the bottom of the abyss.

In September of 1853, sturdy guide and mountain aficionado Michel Carrier, along with a few excellent guides, approached the spot where Balmat had fallen. Here follows is Michel Carrier's account:

Search for Jacques Balmat, 1853,

By Michel Carrier

"We collected all the particulars we could about the place and on our return to the valley, the local guides proposed to me and others to make an expedition to discover, if possible, the remains of Balmat. The proposition was received with great enthusiasm.

Ten of us set out. All the guides of Chamonix would have accompanied us if they could, but we thought our party sufficiently numerous and capable. Our members were united in courage, skill, and prudence.

We crossed the Brevent, descended into the valley of Diosaz, climbed the Col d' Anterne and came down by the chalets to the valley of Sixt. After consulting two of the best guides and gaining all the information we could about the passes, we set off for the valley. The only exit is by steep narrow chamois tracks. Selecting one of these about three miles from the principal village of Sixt, our intrepid guides commenced a rapid ascent along the edge of the precipice.

First, they had to climb grassy slopes, alternating with almost perpendicular rocks. They were obliged to make use of both hands and feet; then to cross several deep ravines before arriving at the foot of a glacier. Surmounted by a wall of rock, they could clearly see down into the dreadful abyss. There lay the remains of the first guide who had ever planted his adventurous foot on the top of Mont Blanc, Jacques Balmat.

It was with deep emotion that our guides regarded the frightful chasm where Balmat had met his tragic fate. Common prudence said to only explore this chasm with their eyes because at every moment sounded avalanches of stone and ice.

Auguste Balmat, one of the great nephews of Balmat, was well known for his bravery. He wanted to be let down into the abyss by a rope. He began the descent by the side, slipping every moment on the rotten schist that broke away under his feet. He had not gone far in this adventurous and daring enterprise when he stopped and gave the signal agreed upon to be drawn up by his companions. Upon his safe withdrawal, he was embraced by the guides in an emotional display. They then all knelt on the last ledge of the precipice as one does by an open grave. It was in truth Jacques Balmat's eternal tomb and it was to be left alone.

We tore ourselves away from this horrible place and returned to Sixt. The next day, we passed by the Chalets of Sales to return to Chamonix.

To convince ourselves that nothing had been neglected, we had a fresh and confidential interview with the chamois hunter who had accompanied Jacques Balmat on his last and fatal expedition.

I had taken a sketch of the scene, which I put before him. He immediately recognized the various localities, and pointed out, without hesitation, the spot from where Jacques Balmat had fallen and met his fate."

What Michel Carrier had long wished for was finally accomplished on August 10th, 1878, when a monument was erected to the Memory of Jacques Balmat by the French Geographical Society and placed in front of the Parish Church at Chamonix.

The universe does not favor greed or cruel ambition; although on the surface it certainly appears to be the case. Perhaps Balmat, having been nicknamed "Mont Blanc" actually believed he was of the mountain and therefore, could not possibly meet the same fate as the others who had perished.

He was wrong.

Surrender

The mountain continued to draw attractors despite the deaths of the skilled and the able and of course, the venerated Jacques Balmat.

Are not the tenacious dreamers the saviors of the world? Their determination is what propels humanity forward, but what profit is there in a mountain climb other than a lofty goal achieved? For many, the ascent of Mont Blanc was the highest vision realized; a destiny fulfilled; an obsession satisfied or a soul rejuvenated or awakened.

I concluded my study of those early mountaineers with the ascent of Paul Verne (the heavily-bearded, dark-haired brother of author Jules Verne) who is believed to have made the fortieth ascent of Mont Blanc.

Ascent of Paul Verne, 1871

"On August 18, 1871, I reached Chamonix with the firm intention of ascending Mont Blanc. I don't care what it costs! The weather, which had been fine all morning, changed suddenly towards noon. Mont Blanc, according to the country phrase, "put on his nightcap and began to smoke his pipe" which, in less fanciful terms, meant that it was covered with clouds and that the snow, drifted about by a strong southeast wind, had formed a long plume on the summit. This plume warned those who dared to climb the mountain.

The following night was very stormy. The wind and rain struggled hard to outdo each other and the barometer, below variable, was provokingly quiet. However, as dawn came on, a few claps of thunder announced a change in the temperature. Soon, the sky cleared. The Brevent and the Aiguilles Rouges reappeared. The wind, veering to the northeast, blew up light fleecy clouds above the Col de Balme, which closes in the Valley of Chamonix on the north. I hailed them as omens of fine weather. Despite these favorable signs, the Chief Guide, declared that we must not dream of making the ascent. This was not very reassuring of my confidence in him and it gave me reason to reflect.

I was accompanied by my friend and fellow countryman, Levesque. A slovenly character with a great thirst for alcohol and a ravenous eater, he was always aware of his physical limitations. Still, he was mad for travelling and a daring pedestrian. He had just returned from an instructive, though often painful, journey in North America. He had already visited the principal cities and was on his way to New Orleans when the war cut his project short and recalled him to France. We met at Aix-les-Bains and resolved to make a trip through Switzerland and Savoy together.

Levesque knew my plans to ascend Mont Blanc. He feared his health would not permit his taking so long a tramp over the glaciers, so it was agreed that he would await my return from Mont Blanc in Chamonix. He would make the traditional visit to the Mer de Glace during my absence.

When he heard that I was going up the Brevent, he did not hesitate to accompany me. The ascent of the Brevent is one of the most interesting trips to be made from Chamonix. We started about seven in the morning. On the way, I asked the guide who had been assigned to me, Edward Ravanal, "Have you ever been up Mont Blanc?"

"Yes, sir," he replied, "once, and that was enough for me. I've no desire to try it again."

"No desire?" I exclaimed. "How can you resist? I feel compelled to do it!"

"The mountain is not in good humor this year. Several attempts have already been made; only two successful ones. The second of those they tried twice. Besides, last year's accident has rather chilled amateurs."

"What accident?"

"You haven't heard? A party of ten started last September for the top of Mont Blanc.

They were seen to reach the summit, then, a few moments after, they vanished into the clouds. When the clouds broke away, no one was seen. Two travelers, with seven guides and porters, were carried away by the wind. The most careful search was made in that area, but their bodies were never recovered. Three were later found one hundred and fifty feet from the summit, near the Petits Mulets. They had all turned to blocks of ice."

My mouth was dry. "But... but these men must have done something imprudent," I protested. "What madness to start such an expedition so late in the season! They should have gone no later than August."

Ravanal pursed his lips and shrugged. He seemed a bit of a shifty character; the type of man who says whatever you want to hear rather than the truth, but still, this story chilled me. In vain, I strove to forget it. Luckily, the sky soon cleared and the beams of a bright sun melted the clouds which still veiled the summit of Mont Blanc and at the same time, those clouds that obscured my mind.

Our ascent up the Brevent was everything that could be desired. On leaving the chalets, we climbed through broken stones and heaps of snow to the foot of a rock known as the Chimney, which we scaled on hands and knees. Twenty minutes later, we were on the top of Brevent. The view was admirable. The chain of

Mont Blanc loomed up in all its majesty. The huge mountain, firmly based on solid strata, seemed to defy the storms that beat against its icy buckler, without ever impairing it; while the mass of needles, peaks, and surrounding mountains bear evident marks of slow decay.

This wonderful spectacle failed to fulfill my ardor and I resolved more firmly than ever to reach the upmost peak. Levesque was equally enthusiastic and began to think that I should not go up Mont Blanc alone. We went back down to Chamonix. The weather was clearing by degrees. The barometer continued to rise slowly; everything looked favorable.

The next day, at dawn, I hurried to the Chief Guide. The sky was cloudless. The wind was hardly stirring a leaf. The range of Mont Blanc, whose principal peaks were gilded by the rays of the rising sun, seemed inviting me to visit. I could not refuse so amiable an invitation.

The Chief Guide declared an ascent feasible and promised me two guides. I left him to choose which guides, but an unexpected event somewhat disturbed my preparations for departure. As I left the office, I met Edward Ravanal, my guide of the previous day.

"Are you going up Mont Blanc?" he asked.

"Yes, of course! Don't you think it's a good day?"

He thought a few moments, and, with a look of constraint, said, "Sir, I took you up Brevent yesterday. I cannot desert you. If you insist upon going up, I will go with you, if you will accept my services. If you accept my offer, I would like you to take my brother, Ambroise Ravanal and my cousin, Gaspard Simond. They are brave young fellows. They don't like such a trip any better than I do, but they won't shirk their work, and I can answer for them as for myself."

Given that I was familiar with Ravanal, I agreed. The matter settled, I went to tell Levesque. I found him sleeping. It was rather hard to rouse him, but by pulling off first the sheets, then the pillows, and finally the mattress, I succeeded in making him understand that I was preparing for my grand journey.

"Well," he said, yawning, "I'll go with you as far as the Grands Mulets and wait for you there."

"Bravo!" I replied. "I have one guide too many and I'll attach him to your person."

About eight the next morning, we began our journey. Upon reaching Pierre Pointue at ten, we encountered a Spanish traveler with two guides and a porter. They started for the Grands Mulets at eleven. We did not get off until noon. We climbed up a steep zigzag path, following the course of the Glacier des Bossons, and running along the base of the Aiguille du Midi.

We advanced slowly, sometimes passing around the crevasses, sometimes crossing them with ladders or on snow-bridges of problematic strength. Here, the rope came into play. It was drawn taut during the dangerous passage in case the snow-bridge should break.

Two years earlier, in 1869, a guide was killed on this very spot; his body hurled into space and crushed on the rocks three hundred feet below. We therefore hastened our steps as much as our inexperience permitted, but, on leaving this dangerous zone, another frightful one awaited us. This was the region of the seracs, huge blocks of ice whose formation is not yet thoroughly understood. The seracs are generally arranged along the edge of a plateau and threaten the whole valley beneath. A simple movement in the glacier, or even a slight vibration of the air, would determine their fall and cause serious accidents.

"Gentlemen, silence here, and move quickly!"

These words, uttered in harsh tones by Ravanal, put an end to conversation. We moved quickly and in silence. Finally, we reached the Junction. Here, the scene assumed a weird character. Crevasses of rainbow hues, slender ice-needles, transparent, overhanging seracs, and little blue-green lakes formed unimaginable worlds. Add to all this the rumbling of torrents below the glacier, the sinister and oft-repeated cracks of masses that break loose and are dashed to the bottom of crevasses, trembling the ground under you, and you will have some idea of these gloomy and desolate districts where life is only revealed in destruction and in death. Here, you wonder why you ever came to such a place.

It was there that I saw a woman or a bird-like woman, who swept in and amongst the cracks, her giant iridescent wings sending harsh blasts of wind that knocked me off my feet. The guides looked at me, puzzled.

"Do you see her?" I asked them.

They looked at me as if I was mad. She grinned at me and sharply cracked her wing, the jolt sending me back against the rocks.

"Too much wine, my friend?" Levesque intoned.

He pulled me to my feet and hurried me on. I was eager to leave this place and held on tight to his knapsack. He was rather pleased to take a guide-like role.

After three hours of scrambling over snow and ice (I was running away from her), we reached the Grands Mulets. A small hut, built by the guides near the summit of the first cliff, and standing 3,050 feet above the level of the sea, offered us shelter and we dined there. I was feeling much better.

"Well," I said to Levesque, "did I exaggerate the splendors of the scene? Do you regret coming this far?"

"So far from regretting it," he replied, "I have decided to go on to the end. You can count on me."

"Very well, but you know that the hardest part is yet to come."

"Pshaw! We'll get the better of it. Meanwhile, let's go look at the sunset."

The sky was wonderfully clear. The Mont Blanc chain alone remained in sunlight and seemed encircled with a golden aureole. Soon, the shadows stole up the Dôme du Goûter and Mont Maudit. We followed this slow and gradual fading of daylight with admiring eyes. It clung some time to the last peak, insensibly inspiring the hope that it would never end. But in a few minutes, everything was dark and the livid and cadaverous hues of death succeeded the brilliant tints of the day. I started to feel fear. *That woman might return.* What if this time, she sent me off the cliff? Why was she picking on me and not the others?

It was foolish to think I could sleep that night. I was absorbed with gloomy thoughts. It was the night before the battle, with this difference: we were not forced to go into the fight. Two conflicting ideas took possession of my mind. Like the ebb and flow of the tide, each one gained in turn. Objections to such a trip were not lacking. What was the use of running such a risk? If I succeeded, what would be the great advantage? If an accident happened, how I would regret going; assuming I was still alive!

My imagination tortured me as every possible catastrophe occurred to me. I heard horrible laughing as if I was being mocked and ridiculed by a thousand different voices. I imagined snow bridges giving way beneath my feet. I was dashed down gaping chasms. I heard the frightful roar of avalanches descending to crush me and I vanished beneath them; a mortal chill seized upon me, and I struggled frantically. A harsh crack sounded, something horrible was approaching.

"Avalanche! Avalanche!" I screamed in terror.

"What is it?!" cried Levesque.

Alas, it was a frantic nightmare, which gave Levesque a great laugh. This prosaic avalanche recalled me to reality and I also laughed at my alarm. The contrary thoughts to such an imagined disaster surfaced and with it, ambitious ideas of a victorious ascent. At these thoughts, my soul grew strong and I awaited the hour of departure, calm.

About one in the morning, voices announced that the time was at hand, but these were the voices of my guides. We sprang up out of bed and dressed quickly. Ambroise Ravanal and his cousin Simond went before to try the road. They carried lanterns for our guidance and hatchets to smooth rough places, and cut steps where necessary. At two, we were tied together and we set out in thick darkness, following the lanterns, borne by the guides who had gone ahead.

There was something solemn about our start. Few words were uttered. The vague unknown awed us, but the new and strange situation excited us and rendered us insensible to our danger. The surrounding landscape was weird and grand. All outlines were indistinct. Huge white masses with black spots shut in the horizon. The heavenly arch shone with unusual brilliancy. At a distance gleamed the swaying lanterns of the guides and the melancholy silence of the night was undisturbed, save for the dry and distant sound of their axes as they hewed out steps in the ice.

We climbed the first acclivity slowly and cautiously, turning towards the base of the Dôme du Goûter. After two hours painful scramble, we reached the first plateau. Having rested a few minutes, we resumed our journey, turning to the left on our way to the Grand Plateau.

Towards four, dawn began to blanch the horizon. We were just mounting the incline that leads to the Grand Plateau. Contrary to custom, Levesque and I had fine appetites. That was a good sign. We sat down in the snow, and made a hearty meal. Our guides were in capital spirits, and felt sure of success. For my part, I thought them rather hasty.

A few moments later, the Spanish traveler's party joined us. We insisted that he should eat something. He refused obstinately. He felt a contraction of his stomach so common in these regions and he was very depressed.

After our rest, we crossed the Grand Plateau and reached the foot of this truly terrible obstacle. The nearer we came, the steeper seemed the incline. Moreover, several crevasses, which we had not noticed, opened at our feet. Nevertheless, we began our laborious ascent. The first guide rough-hewed the steps, the second finished them. We made two steps a minute. The higher we got, the steeper grew the incline. A hailstorm of ice produced by the cutting of the steps, blinded us, and rendered our position still more painful.

Addressing our advance guides, I asked, "How are you going to get us down again?"

Ambroise Ravanal mumbled, "We'll take another road coming down."

Finally, after two hours of violent exertion and after cutting more than four hundred steps in the fearful slope, we reached the top of the Corridor, quite exhausted. We then crossed a slightly inclined plateau of snow and paused to gaze up at Mont Blanc.

"How far away it still is!" cried Levesque.

"And how high!" I noted.

It was indeed discouraging. We rested half an hour, then we continued our road, but we soon felt that the air was not the same. The sun beat down with fiery rays, whose reflection from the snow doubled our torture. The rarefaction of the air began to work cruelly upon us. We advanced slowly, making frequent halts, and at last gained the plateau which crowns the second ridge of the Rochers Rouges. Mont Blanc rose majestic and alone, two hundred feet above us.

Levesque and I were absolutely worn out. As for the Spanish traveler, who had rejoined us on the Corridor, he was insensible to the rarefaction of the air; he had fairly ceased to breathe.

We now began to mount the last stage. We took ten steps and paused from the sheer inability to go on. A painful contraction of the throat made our breathing even more labored. Our legs refused to serve us. I thought of Jacques Balmat's dramatic expression when, in recounting his first ascent, he said that his legs were only held up by his frozen trousers. But a stronger feeling mastered my wearied nature and though my body craved rest, my heart cried out. I stifled a despairing cry and urged on our worn-out frames.

After two hours of superhuman effort, we finally overlooked the whole range. Mont

Blanc was now below us, conquered. It was a little after noon.

The glory of success soon restored our strength. We had conquered the redoubtable peak. We towered above all others and this thought, which Mont Blanc alone can inspire, caused us profound emotion. Ambition was satisfied, and for me at least, a dream was realized.

What a view we had to reward us for our pains. The heaven, still clear, assumed a darker blue. The sun, despoiled of some of his beams, had lost his luster as if partially eclipsed. This effect, due to the rarefaction of the air, was the more apparent. The surrounding plains and mountains were bathed in diffused light. No detail escaped us. The beauty of the spectacle just seemed to increase. It was more magical than a poet's fantasy and more beautiful than any lover.

The temperature was ten degrees above zero. Occasionally, a light easterly breeze was felt. Our guides sat us in a line on the ridge facing Chamonix so that spectators could count us more easily and assure themselves that no one failed to answer the roll-call. Numbers of tourists had gone up the Brevent and the Jardin to watch our ascent. They could all testify to our success.

One is always reluctant to leave a height conquered at the price of such labor, but this was much more than that. This had been the greatest achievement of my life and in that, I felt humbled and deeply satisfied.

The impulse that urged us up; the natural and imperious desire for rule were gone. I felt incredible, soaring emotions that bonded me to its icy banks forever. As we descended, I walked slowly and looked back frequently.

In all human affairs, there are sometimes great efforts. The strength of the effort is the measure of the result. The mountain had infused me with a profound knowledge that I could not impart to others. The effort has to be made in order to be rewarded with this knowledge.

The mountain will not give you anything if you do not surrender your soul to it."

Respect

Those early climbers were profoundly changed by the mountain. Did that happen because it was then all so new? Has the march of time made the spiritual experience of the ascent less felt, if at all? Has Mont Blanc lost its ability to affect humans the way it had on those first forty climbs?

Nowadays, there seems to be a certain disrespect of this peak. Not even the best season for climbing can be honored. Climbers toy with their lives by going when the season is most deadly, as in February, 2013 when two Lithuanian climbers were stranded for three days and three nights at 12,795 feet near the summit of Les Droites on Mont Blanc's massif.

The two had been pinned down by winds up to 75 mph, temperatures of minus 22 degrees and constant snow, preventing a rescue team from reaching them at their shelter 492 feet below the summit.

On Friday morning at 6 a.m., the PGHM (rescue team) received a text saying that one climber had succumbed to the cold. On Saturday, another text was sent from the surviving climber, saying he had dug a snow hole and was safe, but had run out of gas for his stove.

A rescue helicopter was sent to the area on Sunday morning, but high winds prevented a rescue attempt. The helicopter was sent again Sunday afternoon, but by then it was too late. The visual sighting of the remaining climber confirmed that he had left the snow hole, had somehow fallen and was hanging from the end of his rope.

What is it about people that they think they can demand from this mountain whatever they want? Is it their goal to achieve its peak in the off-season to recount a story of great achievement or is it their goal to test if they are indeed mortal?

Unfortunately, the tourists, skiers and climbers flock here and desecrate the slopes with pollutants and human waste. This commune is simply too overpopulated. They cannot conceive of this sacred giant. They are too self-absorbed to listen to its lessons or appreciate its soulful existence. It is merely another goal in their climbing career.

In an attempt at preservation and protection, the Mont Blanc massif is being put forward as a potential World Heritage Site due to its uniqueness and cultural importance. It is considered the birthplace and symbol of modern mountaineering, but for us, of course, Mont Blanc is much more significant than a peak on which to climb.

Love

It could be argued that the sensation of lightness of being, the emotional toll, the reflection on one's life and the strange sensations experienced by these ascenders is merely due to the effects of the mountain air. However, I have been to the Himalaya range and the Andes and in neither case did I experience the penetration of my soul as with Mont Blanc.

The great guru of Europe forcefully puts life into a perspective that is felt and experienced second by second. Does the White Mountain make a better human being? From the published accounts of the early ascenders, it certainly stirred something in them they had never experienced before. I know I have changed and so has Ana.

Those who ascend the mountain rise towards the light. When at an elevation of five or six thousand feet, the climber emerges from the shifting ocean of mists and vapors and sees the peaks and the glaciers soaring above him into (hopefully) a serene day. On the contrary, when the climber is caught in the darkness of night, the living soul of the mountain is felt in its harsh reality. But it is night, not necessarily death. In its mighty upheaval, these piercing mountain peaks are not deliberately harsh.

The Alps have their own sorrows and hold the graves of the ambitious, the weak and the daring. Here, Nature prevails with a higher energy; attracting, tempting and inducing all men and women to climb upon its body. The intoxication is grand and I am one of its claimed victims.

Here, you see the fullness of its magical, voluptuous, and sinister forces. Its great bazaars of jewels are exposed to the desires of men and women. Its price is the cost of one's life. The Alps, in their seductive agency, marvelous and profound at night, in sweet repose during the day, beckon again and again, sometimes claiming bodies, but always claiming souls.

Ana seems sheltered by our life here in the mountain air, shut in with her own fanciful thoughts and studies. She appears to know little of the world's labors, of the immensity of its awful reality. She now has a vivid and delicate sense of life and does not succumb to the confusions and chaos of day-to-day life anymore. She aids the climbers, serves as a docent of the mountain and is always pointing out the majesty of its existence.

Wife and wise friend, mother of our beloved Sean, universal comforter, Ana, you were created to be the happiness and the salvation of many. Love will not fail you. You are love.

In this contrived and concocted existence humans have created, it is easy to separate man from Nature, certain members of society from the greater humanity, but here in this mountain region, man, woman, beast, mountain - all of Nature - are one great family.

The deadline for the assignment is long over and I have instead written this book. We have chosen to remain in Chamonix. We are not hiding. We are not in a world of distraction. We are keenly living, more aware than ever before. The healing balm of Nature serves us well and in turn, we dedicate our lives to her longevity.

Despite the financial hardship of remaining here, our marriage now is always blazing with life and renewal as we spend time on the mountain. I see more clearly, I feel more intensely, I laugh more richly and I love more deeply. That is what Mont Blanc gave me.

Calmness of mind gives relief from grief and realization of what truly matters. It is one of the beautiful jewels of wisdom. Thoughtful reflection and growth has led me to this much longed-for sense of peace and keen awareness of life and purpose.

Until my last moment on Earth, this giant bald hermit will have my undying gratitude.